The Last
Evacuee

REFLECTIONS UPON
A CHANGING WINDOW

a memoir

The Last Evacuee

REFLECTIONS UPON
A CHANGING WINDOW

a memoir

LILIAN & STEPHEN WHITE

*The author is contributing five per cent of his
profits from the sale of this book to the RNLI*

First impression: 2014

Cover design: Y Lolfa
Cover photograph and illustrations: Stephen White

ISBN: 978 184771 830 3

Published and printed in Wales
on paper from well-maintained forests by
Y Lolfa Cyf., Talybont, Ceredigion SY24 5HE
website www.ylolfa.com
e-mail ylolfa@ylolfa.com
tel 01970 832 304
fax 832 782

Contents

Foreword

by Stephen White

THIS IS THE story of the life of my mother, Lilian. It includes important events from my mother's earliest times to the present but it concentrates on her experiences during the Second World War.

As a young girl, Lilian's modest world was turned upside down and all that she knew and loved was taken away from her. She travelled hundreds of miles away from her home in London to live, for the first time, with a middle-class family – the Morgans. Lilian now found herself in strange surroundings, where the privileged lives of those around her were even more exceptional than she could have ever imagined. The head of the household was nominated to be Lord Mayor; his wife was awarded a medal from King George. The wife's sister, who also lived in the house, had been a missionary in Africa.

Lilian attended the local church for long periods and then returned to a household where the stricter Quaker beliefs held sway.

She indulged her carefree spirit within the extraordinary, exciting and wonderful environment that surrounded her new house but, for doing so, she nearly paid with her life – twice!

She entered a world where high expectations and hard work were never far away. She saw places that she had never seen before and experienced sensations that she had never felt before. She learned that trivial offences were treated harshly. She was shocked by one new way of life, yet was inspired by another.

This is an account of both happy and sad times. There are visits by royalty and famous thespians. There are moments of humour and joy but there are also darker, tragic episodes. It is the story of a journey through life, made most unusual by a unique collection of events and most memorable by the rarest and most inspirational of characters.

Introduction

SEVERAL YEARS AGO, Lilian began writing the account of her wartime experiences, called 'The Changing Window'. It was about a period in her life that she found to be very traumatic. After completing her first draft, she was advised to write more about how unprivileged she had been in her early years and contrast that with the time that she spent with the Morgan family.

As she wrote more, her daughter Janice helped with the editing. However, Janice got married and left the household to start her own family before the project was completed. It then fell to me to assist my mother with her story. As time passed, my mother became less able to do many things and eventually stopped writing.

Just after the turn of the new millennium, she succumbed to her frailty. If there was anything else that she could have added to her book, it now appeared forever lost. It was at this point that I reached a very sad and apparently insurmountable dilemma: I had in my possession half of a story that I felt was certainly worthy of completion but the author was no longer there to help me. I did not wish to 'fill in the gaps' by making things up, lest the reader might construe that what was already written, was fiction but I could not help asking myself how else I could possibly complete the book – a task that now seemed impossible.

Eventually, though, I slowly came to realise that my mother had not taken all of the missing chapters with her. She had left many notes about things that were still to be written about. I found them useful and I was able to construct some of her story from those.

I could also rely on what Lilian had previously said about her wartime experiences, and information from her relatives was to prove useful as well although I shall leave such details out right now lest the reader be forewarned about what the expect – when my mother was not! The last chapter sheds more light on the way this book has been constructed – and includes... well... as I just said – lest the reader be forewarned – I shall leave it there. (But it's good though! You wait and see!)

Some of the names of people and places have been changed, in order to protect the identities of certain individuals. Chapters where the actual names of real people are used within the story are subject to the subheading of 'improvised dialogue' where events generally occurred as depicted but where most dialogue was previously unrecorded by my mother. Subheadings 'dramatization' are used where, although events very possibly happened, there is a higher degree of uncertainty surrounding them.

Finally, on a more grammatical vein, I feel that I should just explain why I completed this endeavour by writing in the first person, not the third. I wrote, for instance, that she said, "I did this" or "I thought that" when it might have been more historically correct to have written, "she *probably* did this" or "she *might* have done that", as some of what I was writing was based upon estimates and assumptions. However, I thought that the book would be easier to read if it was spared the many convoluted descriptions of assumptions that I was making and it was completed instead in the first person. I hope that the reader understands that it was done with sincerity, to facilitate the understanding and appeal of the story, and not to compromise its basic integrity.

1

The world I would leave behind

In remembrance of my home, family and friends

I LEANT FORWARD and gazed out of my small bedroom window – in the little room that had been mine for the past few months, atop possibly the finest hotel in a town that had been my home for over five years – and contemplated the turbulent scene before me. For as far as I could see, great, grey autumn clouds had come above and all around me and an irritated, churning, roaring sea scratched and lapped insatiably at the hotel's imposing, defiant cliff foundations fifty feet below.

I brushed my fair hair back, away from my eyes. Damp locks, made wet from the rain only minutes before, were

busily casting their cool tears upon my forlorn face; it was proving futile to wipe away their small contribution to the broken visage. I watched an angry nature spellbound and stared blankly towards the horizon, through the sheets of hard hail impatiently throwing themselves at the other side of the battered window. Mesmerised, I reached out, to rest my tired hand gently upon the animated chilled pane, to be gradually transported back, to another time and another place. I was returning, in my mind, to London – the city of my birth. There, in 1929, my young eyes first opened to perceive, in delight, a world of innocence and enchantments – a place so draped in charm and magic that a new, vibrant imagination would most easily conceive the wildest of adventures within it, and where all the present encumbrances of a maturing life were yet to be.

Not far from the centre of the great metropolis, I was to spend my first ten, relatively happy years living with my parents, my brother Arthur, and my three sisters: Doris, Nancy and Rhona. In those days, close relatives often lived quite near to each other and with my mother's parents residing in the next street, ours proved to be no exception.

I was born probably at home and probably with a midwife in attendance. Unfortunately, my family did not consider posterity and left details of the whole event unrecorded. Nevertheless, into the world of the Depression I popped, immediately taking my place as the second of my mother's many children.

I was immediately held firmly and given a slap on the back. I felt that it was a particularly brutal start to my life, being beaten just for being born, and suspected that my parents were just preparing me for hard times ahead. I have been told since that it was the usual practice to help a newly born infant to start breathing and that I should not have taken it personally. Fortunately, as far as I can remember, it only happened on that one occasion in my life.

My working-class family soon moved about half a mile away, to a corner house in Islington, north London. Not long afterwards we moved again, this time to the top floor of a tenement house in Weston Rise. The property was rented from a private landlord. It was not very well-endowed, having no running hot water, no bathroom and no proper bath to put in it, anyway!

My first proper home and bath-time terrors

For me, the early terrors of all-over body cleansing took place in a small, portable tin bath. The first time that I was to use it – and I was still unaware of its purpose – I remembered what I had glimpsed in the kitchen when my mother was cooking. Some of her food had been placed inside a saucepan, whereupon water was added and heated up until steam was seen coming from it. After a while, the food was taken out and my family ate it.

Now, an object similar to that saucepan – only without the long handle – was placed on the floor. Then my mother began bringing in some water – some of it steaming – and pouring it into the tin receptacle, a container that was particularly conducive to my size and shape! My mind began racing. I quickly took a frantic hold of my precious shapes, colours and touchy things, and began to play with them as much as possible. I was trying to distract my mother and myself. I was hoping that she would somehow forget why she was carrying out her (presumably fiendish) preparations and put everything away again, but it appeared to be of no use.

She ceremoniously bent down, placed her elbow into the water and then stood upright again. She now seemed ready to throw me into it. As her determined figure approached me – with those menacing, outstretched arms – I tried playing 'throwing the shapes away, then grabbing them again', hoping that she would see me doing something important and leave me alone, but all was to no avail.

"Come along, Lily," she said, cunningly trying to urge me to go quietly into the water but she had said similar things when she was cooking the *other* food. "Ooh, you're a lovely carrot," I am sure I once heard her say.

I began screaming and crying almost constantly throughout the whole new, unpleasant experience. My precious toys were cruelly taken from my hands and placed upon my cot; my clothes were forcibly removed. The time for decisive action had come. I was lifted up and out of my cot, and held over the great pot. Way below me, something was bobbing about on the water. It seemed that I had missed her adding the vegetables even *before* she had started steaming the main course! I tried every trick in the book: I dribbled, wriggled, screamed and cried.

Nothing that I did changed anything with the hard woman when, ever so gently, she lowered me into the lukewarm water, to give me my first experience of being covered in the liquid all of the way up to my waist. Straight away, I was given the floating thing to play with – as a crafty distraction, I surmised – but I was determined to escape and immediately pushed it under the water as I made my daring bid for freedom.

At once, before I could go for the breakout, the device mockingly came back to the surface. I knew I had to keep the object below the surface and bashed it several times with my hands. The principles of mass, volume, displacement and buoyancy were difficult to comprehend as I continued hitting the thing with all of my limbs and all of the energy that I could muster. It seemed to work but just when it appeared that I had finally succeeded in keeping the floating thing beneath the water, my mother cunningly forced a wet flannel into each of my ears. As the soapy water did its job of removing my capacity to hear, my mother slyly utilised my moments of sensory deprivation by sneaking up behind me and then smothering the great flannel all over my face as well.

As everything began getting too much for me, I resorted to crying again in the hope that that would bring the whole terrible experience to an end. I had now lost my senses of sound *and* sight. If only I could have been denied my sense of taste instead, I thought, after my open, wailing mouth attracted some of the soapy flannel's water.

Eventually – possibly through some belated form of regret – my mother pulled me from that cruel pot of pain. She dried me with the patting and rubbing of a towel that seemed to say how sorry she was to have caused me to cry almost constantly for those last twenty minutes. She awkwardly put new, clean clothes on me and then gently placed me back in my cot.

As she left me, she seemed to give solemn praise for a divine guidance that had concluded an episode so regrettable, parting as she did with the words, "Thank God that's over."

Any fears that all had been a cunning preparation for some dreadful mealtime experience were dispelled as I lay exhausted from screaming but determined to defeat the floating thing if I should ever again, unfortunately, encounter the menace of the giant water pot.

What a day! What was going to happen to me next, I wondered, as I effortlessly shut my eyes and slid back down into the colourful land of Nod, from whence I had come only a few hours earlier.

The young explorer

After several weeks, I was taken to see the world outside of the room. I sat inside my sister's old pram, beside the steps of my house, and looked all around at the new, strange surroundings. I leant over – away from the pram's overhanging shade – and saw the sun for the first time. It strangely hurt my eyes and I had to look away quickly. That was a shame. It was warm and the source of the light that had shone into my room. Now, I could almost bathe beneath it and be a part of its natural glory. It was appearing from behind one dull-grey line of identical terraced houses. It would eventually set behind our house – part of another dull-grey line of identical terraced houses. Nature seemed so wonderful!

When my mother started pushing my pram along the pavement, I became more excited, as I realised that I could now travel hundreds of yards outside and explore more of my environment.

Every so often, some of the women down our street left their doorsteps to smile at me and tickle me beneath my chin. It made me laugh, not because they had not realised that I had already been tickled that day but because of the tickles themselves. I could never have had too many tickles... unless, of course, I was trying to eat... or sleep. Then it would have become a bit of a nuisance!

On my journey around the streets, I became aware of some people playing strange and wonderful games on them. I wanted to join in but experience had taught me that it was very difficult remaining upright for more than a second or two and that, obviously, only the most practised were allowed out to walk on the streets unaided.

Suddenly, non-human creatures – animals – flying in the sky, landed nearby! Other people – a little bigger than I was and able to walk quite quickly – fearlessly chased after them. They were unable to capture any. I desperately wanted to help them with their thrilling endeavours but my inadequate legs prevented me. Another creature, which was moving about on all fours, stopped by a post and raised one of its legs. It then deposited some liquid, lowered its leg and came towards me. I let out a scream as it passed me by.

A round object suddenly came bouncing towards me, chased by a mother and her child. My mother stopped the object and handed it to me, explaining that it was a ball. She told me to throw it back, so l let go of it and it rolled down and away, back to the child. Had he not picked it up, I felt sure that it would have rolled on forever!

Suddenly, I heard 'clip-clop' noises behind me that got louder and louder. I stared as a huge beast, pulling what looked like a big pram behind it, passed me. On top of the 'pram' were lots of barrel-shaped objects. A man appeared to be sitting on one at the front and holding onto some ropes attached to the beast.

What a strange world existed, I thought, just outside my room: a blinding light, terrifying creatures, giant 'prams' of barrels, and objects that seemed to roll on forever, when pushed. What a world!

My street – the fully grown toddler's playground

When I became a fully grown toddler, I made friends with other East End toddlers, and played with them up and down my short, cobble-stoned street. Our games tended to require the smallest financial outlay, for we were of very limited means. My home had some marbles in it but little else of any use, as was my small stone backyard. I therefore had to become quite resourceful and make use of whatever was available in the street.

I once found a large, old, abandoned bicycle wheel (that was not attached to a large, old, abandoned bicycle) and began rolling it along the ground with my hand. When I started striking along the top of it with a stick instead, it became easier to keep the wheel moving and less likely that it would fall over but I then had to run faster just to stay with it.

It is generally very flat in London, which was probably a boon or I might never have kept up with the wheel at all. My new prized toy would then have gone speeding away downhill with poor little toddler Lilian racing along in hot pursuit... *"Come back wheel!"*

Something else that I did, was to save empty jam jars and

then give them to a particular man with a merry-go-round who occasionally came down our street. He let me have a few minutes on his ride for every jar that I gave him. It was a wonderful and unique experience to go round and round in circles in the middle of our street to the accompaniment of gay music; it always made this little girl's afternoon.

Mother... and her eternal housework

My mother was a short lady with dark eyebrows, dark blue eyes and hair that was set in deep waves. She wore floral aprons, and her sleeves were permanently rolled up in preparation for the work that she would be doing all day around our home.

With no modern appliances (and a complete lack of electricity to power them anyway), all of the housework that she did was necessarily slow and laborious. She nearly always seemed to be scrubbing the wooden stairs, cleaning our drab-coloured linoleum floors and doing the laundry.

Holes quickly developed in clothes that were rubbed too much during the washing, which then required lengthy sewing repairs. Badly damaged articles were used as patches on other damaged clothes or as rags. On very special occasions, they were extravagantly used to make rag dolls, although such a use of rags had to be limited; after all, we had to have *something* to wear!

Father

When I was born, my father was a journeyman painter but, within a few years, he changed his occupation and created quite a successful fruit and vegetable business in nearby Chapel Street. Several people were employed by him. Considering that there was the Great Depression at the time, his finances never suffered too badly.

He was tall, with fair hair and – like me – he had blue eyes. He dressed well in comparison to the rest of the family and was always to be seen wearing the clean shirts that he demanded, and received, from my mother.

I soon started to recognise that those demands and the inequality of his attire compared to his family's, were just the result of his nasty character – one that was just like his brother's. The frequent fights into which the pair got themselves went well towards their bad reputations.

While I had been getting on well with my mother so far, my relationship with my father was distant at the best of times. I was disregarded by him. He thought children were unimportant and undeserving of his attention. He never put himself out to praise anything that I did well; in fact, I cannot even remember him being bothered to say "Hello" to me. To him, I might as well have not existed.

Perhaps the 'demon drink' was partly to blame. My father was an alcoholic and spent most evenings across the main road, satisfying his habit at the public house. Sometimes my mother went with him.

When I was only a few years old, I was once left standing outside my father's house of inebriation, patiently waiting for my parents to emerge. As I surveyed the drab exterior, I heard loud voices from within. Soon after, boisterous songs were emitted.

"Would you like a taste of my drink?" a kind man enquired as I quietly stood there reflecting upon a parental love so sorely missed.

I shook my head, declining the offer. Tears began to well up in my eyes. I hated the scene before me and I had had enough. I turned on my heels. From that moment, I was determined never to wait in vain for my parents again.

My aunts and Mr Bridge

My family occupied the two rooms on the top floor of our house. My mother's sisters – Freda and Eleanor – lived below us on the first floor. In the two rooms on the ground floor, there was Mr Bridge. He was a bachelor and the friend of an aunt – at least I *think* that he was just the friend of an aunt! He was a nice man for whom I ran errands. He used to tell my mother what he wanted – for instance, bread and marmalade – and then my mother would tell *me*. I would then run down to the local shop to get it. Mr Bridge gave me one penny each time I completed an errand.

I took my reward to the local sweet shop and bought as much as I could with it. I frequently chose Golliwog Toffee Bars, as they only cost one farthing, so I could afford more of those than most other sweets.

Money and salvation
My mother grew up through hard times. She remembered the dreadful conditions of the workhouses, which once cast grievous shadows over this nation. I do not think that she ever entered their 'accommodation' but her family knew enough about them and those who frequented them, to do their best to avoid passing through their doors at all costs, even when things at home seemed dire.

There came an early period in my mother's life, when she and her family were very poor but they were kept from extreme hunger by the food given away by the God-sent charity workers of the Salvation Army.

When I was very young, I too had good cause to be grateful to the Salvation Army. Although we still had a roof over our heads, we did not have much food left to eat or money left to buy any more. We were in need and the 'Sally Army' staved off our hunger with their warm soup and other sustenance. For their kind acts of charity, I promised myself that I would repay them later, when I could.

Sometimes, the meals that we had at home were not very nutritious but they usually cured my hunger. For instance, after a meal had been cooked, slices of bread were sometimes dipped into the used fat in the frying pan in order to make 'dipped-in'. These sandwiches of fatty bread were cheap, warm and, surprisingly, very tasty.

Whenever the flow of money into the house started to diminish, as was often the case, the local pawnbrokers saw my father's familiar face again. The same old family 'heirlooms' were temporarily swapped once more for a little money in the hope that better times in the near future would enable them to be bought back later, albeit for a much larger sum. Unfortunately, my father was not able to reclaim everything that he pawned.

I eventually noticed that my mother and father were starting to row with increasing frequency. It appeared to me to have something to do with money. At the time, for example, I could not help wondering why the biscuits that my mother sent me out to buy had to be the cheap broken ones instead of the more expensive unbroken ones, whereas my father was less troubled by similar unpleasant compromises. He definitely seemed better off, financially, than we were. Everything became much clearer when it was revealed that he had been spending a lot of his money on himself and other women whom he entertained. I was not aware of this for several years, although that did finally explain the disparity between his appearance and his family's, and why he always had so little money left on him to feed and clothe us.

Comings and goings

When I was about two years old, my new brother Arthur arrived. About three years later, my father walked out on his wife and us children, presumably to live with one of his many female friends. I was not to miss him.

Not long afterwards, my mother became friendly with another man. He had dark, receding hair and was rather round faced and short. After a while, my next sister, Nancy, duly joined the family.

Within a year or so of Nancy's birth, my mother's

fair-weather partner vacated the scene and, soon after, my father returned. With more children than ever to look after, my mother might have been grateful for the one extra adult again in the home but his homecoming appeared more for his own benefit than anyone else's and, unfortunately, there had been no change in his character.

Gold!

When I was young, my mother told me that she had a dozen gold sovereigns hidden away for an emergency. Perhaps that was just her way of making me feel less insecure, lest I might be worried about one of our many hard times that she felt sure were to lie ahead. I never saw the coins; I have always wondered just how she could have acquired them. It did make me wonder, though, if she really *did* have a little 'gold mine' stashed away somewhere!

School!

When I was old enough, my mother took me along to the infants' school at the end of my road, where I was to be kept all day and forced to learn things. With a "Goodbye, Lily. Be good," and a kiss on the cheek, my mother left me standing beside a classroom, abandoning me with all of the other new and confused pupils.

A strict-looking teacher, whom I saw hovering at the front of her classroom, bade us to enter. I decided to be brave and slowly entered the room with my fellow pupils. I tried to stay in the centre of the mass of young humanity, as I knew that there was always safety in numbers and that the teacher would most likely go for any stragglers or those on the outside first. She looked ready to deal with any rebellious behaviour from any erstwhile toddler. We little ones all quickly accepted the situation and submitted to it; resistance seemed futile.

We were all told to find a vacant desk and then stand behind it, so we each made our way towards one of *several* vacant desks and stood behind those (we correctly assumed that she did not expect us all to find, and then squeeze behind, just the one desk).

When instructed to do so, we all sat down behind our desks, on chairs that were suitably constructed to hold our small frames. My class settled itself and began listening intensely and silently to the teacher. Fidgeting was discouraged and when we had something to say, whether it was to ask a question or proffer an answer, we were told to raise our hand first. At all other times we were not allowed to speak in the class. So began my education.

Edward VIII and all that
I was only about six when the scandal broke about Prince Edward's affair with an American divorcee, Mrs Simpson. Their relationship was ridiculed in a popular song of the day. The prince, preferring the love of Mrs Simpson to the title King of England, abdicated. I found the sacrificing of his inheritance quite moving.

Children's clubs and more games
I eventually belonged to various children's clubs at the local Baptist church. Frequent parties were held there, lots of games were played and there were usually plenty of lovely jelly and jam tarts as well, for the indulgence of all.

When a large complex for children was opened a few streets away, I went along to see it. It was the largest recreation place that I had ever seen, incorporating many slides, swings and sand pits. There were sections for painting and there were also cheap refreshments available.

Another new arrival – Doris
In 1936, my new sister, Doris, was born. She was a nice, attractive girl, with a round face, big bright eyes and a cute nose. She was not in perfect health though, as her left eye

was permanently very close to her nose, which made her sometimes go cross-eyed. She needed an operation to remedy it but she was not going to suffer that until later in her life. For the time being, she would become my new close friend and mean more to me than any of my other siblings would. That was especially true in Rhona's case. She was born the year before I was and was now becoming like a stranger in the house.

Possibly because Doris had a slight impairment, she was treated a little more specially by my mother than the rest of us children were. Unlike us, she regularly had her hair washed with rainwater and was given the luxury of Amari shampoo. Afterwards, my mother sometimes set Doris' hair in special ways in order to make her look especially pretty, such as by adding the odd curls or including a bun-style arrangement somewhere.

Royal visitors

One day, I was thrilled to see Princesses Elizabeth and Margaret arriving in a coach, in order to visit the children's complex. As the resplendent party – in immaculate brimmed straw hats and pastel-shaded coats – left their royal carriage, a huge chorus of cheers rose up. Some inconsiderate spectators behind me pushed forwards to get a better view of the unfolding events. I was then squashed and pushed back by the police and other security people. (I was not actually pushed back after first being squashed – the squashing was merely a lamentable consequence of being pushed back!)

As Elizabeth, Margaret and their entourage disappeared into a large building close by, little union flags waving aloft were lowered and the attendant mass of spectators – me included – all too quickly began returning once more to our generally rather dull and matter-of-fact existences.

A new school

As my infant years slowly drifted away, I started attending the local junior school, which was about half a mile away. On one occasion, after talking in class when I should not have, I was immediately punished by the teacher by having my mouth washed out with soap and water. I tended to behave a bit better after that!

Learning the ropes

As I was growing up, I found myself becoming a bit of a tomboy and my games often reflected that newer and more boisterous character of mine. The streets were generally very safe for playing on. Horses and carts were slow, and the motor cars, which were faster, were very infrequent. Their appearances were as rare as their reasons were for coming to our area. If they did ever come, their occupants were considered rich and they were viewed quite enviously, almost as curiosities... *Ooo...*

We made do with whatever could be found discarded and lying around. A short piece of rope could be used for skipping. Discovering longer old ropes meant that either taller (and probably older) people could play skipping with us as well or we would just hang them from lampposts and swing from them (we would swing from the *ropes* that is, not the tall people who would not play with us).

Opposite my home was a firm that belonged to a brewery. Outside one entrance, on a pavement, stood a gas lamppost that had a horizontal bar either side of it. This made an ideal swing after we threw a rope – sometimes with an improvised wooden seat attached – over one of the bars.

Next door to where I lived was a yard where my friends and I – in borrowed clothes and shoes from my mother – performed plays in front of other children. We charged a halfpenny for this.

"Get out!" was the frequent shout from a window above

the yard, where an elderly, grey-haired lady lived. We would then make a hasty exit, running away in all directions, only to return a few days later.

Crime

Apart from the dreadful acts that sometimes took place in the adjacent yard, there were not really any other bad dramatic incidents being carried out in our neighbourhood.

House security is something worth mentioning, though. People could leave their front doors unlocked where we lived and that was not because they had little worth stealing, although they did have little worth stealing (possibly because they had left their front doors unlocked!). In our case, my family had little worth stealing, yet we locked our front doors anyway, just to be on the safe side.

Saturday morning tuppenny rushes and Shirley Temple's hairdos

On Saturday mornings, my mother gave me 2d. so that I could race to the local cinema with all of the boys and girls from the nearby streets in what was called the 'tuppenny rush'. Before the main feature started, we would usually be shown one or two shorts (the 'shorts' that we sat looking at were short pictures – episodes from cliff-hanger serials such as *Flash Gordon* – not articles of clothing).

The films featured stars like Mickey Rooney and Judy Garland. If Shirley Temple was in a film, many of us girls would pay particular attention to her (usually curly) hairdo and then rush back home afterwards, to copy the hairstyle. As a ten year old, my natural hair was otherwise short, straight and with a fringe.

Father leaves home... again!

When I was about nine or ten, my father left home for a second time. I could only assume that his absence would be permanent. Without his income, my mother was forced to go out and find employment. This tended to be hard, low-paid cleaning work. She ended up on her hands and knees, for instance, scrubbing the steps of the local hospital.

My toy collection

One of my favourite possessions (albeit virtually the only one) was a little rag doll. It might not have been immaculately dressed – I had only a few rags in which to dress her – but it was something of mine that I could cherish and play with. I could dress her in the finest pink rags available. I could put her in what was meant to be a grand coach, pulled by what was meant to look like a team of thoroughbred stallions, and transport her to what was supposed to be reminiscent of a magnificent palace. There she could sit down and take care of her own little bundle of rags, her 'new-born princess' – my own little rag-based creation.

I imagined a world for her where she was conducting herself at a royal court; at other times imprisoned in a tower and then saved by a brave knight; or surviving on a desert island; or just having her friends around for tea. I used whatever I could to conjure up a complete environment for her and let her realm become mine. I could cuddle and love my little rag doll, made from the little that we had. Whatever the situation was that I put her in, I escaped into it as well – in my mind.

After Doris was born and she too was considered old and responsible enough to look after her own rag doll, my make-believe world of the doll in my bedroom became more pleasant, as strong, realistic and permanent bonds of friendship materialised for the sweet little cherished things in their beloved kingdom of rags.

Twilight at home

The setting of the sun at the day's end depressingly marked the return of virtual darkness to streets that were barely lit by the flickering glow from lines of inadequate gas lamps. Individuals – young and old – had to choose whether to remain outside in the vacant, long shadows or retreat despondently once more into the gloom of their own murky homes, lit only by the defiant glows from the odd gas flames, desperate yellow candlelight and the meagre glimmering incandescence of a small lounge fire.

My friends and I tended to go back to our houses as darkness fell, to amuse ourselves throughout the twilight hours with our limited resources of toys and games.

Natural illumination and heat came in the morning, with the rising of the sun. Like modern-day troglodytes, the inhabitants of the nearby houses and I could emerge once more, blinking and squinting at the God-given source of brilliant radiance. Until then, many like us sometimes just listened to the radio, which was an ideal pastime, as you did not need any light to enjoy that; you only had to find the 'on' button (and then the tuning and volume knobs).

Of course, we also did not need light in order to do several other things. To sing, for instance, requires no light at all, although not everyone in our area suddenly started singing as soon as the sun went down.

Nor should it be inferred that silent people in the gloomy local houses were liable to be walked into by the other occupants unless they continued making sounds like singing or talking or even playing a musical instrument. If that had been the case, then I do not think that anyone would have managed to get to sleep before well after midnight, considering the racket that would have been going on!

Arthur often stayed out late, doing *something* until well after sunset and after the public houses had opened (although he was, as yet, far too young to frequent them). Doris, Nancy and I would escape into a world of play in the bedroom. Our mother would relax, perhaps by listening to the radio, sometimes while sewing garments back together if there was still sufficient light left for her to see what she was doing.

In the nearby public houses, drinkers were quickly spending their hard-earned cash as closing time fast approached, probably moaning to the landlord as all of their money, valuable drinking time and sobriety conspired to leave them all at the same time.

And so they passed away, their twilight hours. Then something came on the radio, and I was taught how to spell Czechoslovakia.

2

End of an era

Gas?

HAVING MANY FRIENDS and various activities, I became quite a confident child. I felt free to please myself as to where I went and what I did when I actually got there! However, when I was about nine years of age my life began to change dramatically. Preparations for less certain times ahead began to cast an ominous shadow over my carefree youth – a liberty that had seemed so untroubled and forever guaranteed. I was not too aware of the reasons for what was happening; someone mentioned it was something to do with the Germans.

In the local park, for instance, little trench systems were dug, apparently for hiding in during an air raid. At the same time, most disquietingly, gas masks began to be issued.

I had to go with my family to the town hall in order to be given one of the new masks. When I queued up for mine, I watched ahead of me as some very young children were given special masks with comical red, floppy noses attached. Elsewhere, surreal, dehumanized forms – groups of children who had chosen to keep their masks on for a while, unsure of what to do with their huge, awkward rubber and metal proboscises – curiously and slowly moved unassuredly around each other. The wearers ominously expressed delight and relief upon removing those masks a few minutes later.

I eventually made it to the front of the queue and gave my name to the man in charge of the issuing of masks. He took one from his collection (one without a silly nose) and told

me to stick out my chin. He then placed the mask under my chin and pulled the black contraption up and over my head until it gripped me tightly all around my face.

After a minute or so of pulling and pushing down on my head with the mask, he politely enquired, "Can you still breathe?"

I was still vertical and conscious, so I thought that that should have been a rather massive clue. I was hoping that his question was one of philanthropic care rather than homicidal curiosity.

"Yes," I happily replied, hoping that my response would

please, rather than disappoint him. All the time, I was doing my best to ignore the new sensation of almost being suffocated by the skin of smelly rubber that was clenching me tightly.

"Pardon?" he asked.

"Yes, *sir*," I said, believing him to have taken some sort of offence at not being answered with a proper address. I did not realise that with the design of the mask that I was wearing – with my ears partly exposed but my mouth covered – it was a lot easier for me to hear him than it was for him to hear me.

"OK then. There you are. I'll take it off you now," he said, attempting to remove the mask and, unintentionally, some of my facial extremities at the same time. After he removed it, he put it in its cardboard box and looped the string of it over me, so that it would not get lost on the way home.

"Now look after it, Lilian. Don't lose it, will you?" he warned.

"No, sir," I replied, fearing that I would have to go through the entire fitting procedure again if I did.

As the remaining members of my family received their masks, I wiped not a little sweat from my hot brow and was thankful that, at least for the time being, I did not have to wear the mask for a *real* emergency.

New little buildings to play in
I became the close friend of a girl called Jeanette. She was taller than I was. She had large dimples in her cheeks and she sported thick, dark-brown, wavy hair.

Her family – clearly better off than we were – lived in a large house on the corner of my street. They occupied all of the substantial property. We, by contrast, only had the limited access to our one floor. Because they also enjoyed a long front garden, they were entitled to one of the new, mass-produced, government-supplied outbuildings.

One day, several trucks began unloading pieces of curved, corrugated sheeting onto various gardens down Jeanette's street. Many of the older recipients inexplicably appeared particularly glum.

When all of the pieces were delivered and the vehicles left, I went down to see Jeanette. Standing with her was her father, looking rather blankly at his shed-like collection of components. In one hand, he was holding the leaflet of instructions that he had just been given. He was scratching his head with his other hand – almost as though he was doing a Stan Laurel impression.

"Right then. Let's see what we've got to do with this," he said, boldly studying the leaflet.

I looked at Jeanette, who looked at me, and then at the corrugated metal sheets lying on the ground. In awe, both Jeanette and I then stared up at her dad.

After a minute or so, the gentleman exclaimed, "Let's go and have a nice cup of tea." He retreated, defeated, indoors and took his disappointed daughter with him. I looked once more at the challenging pile of various pieces of metal on their lawn. Then I went back to my home as well.

A few days later, I went down to see my friend again, who now sat proudly upon the couple of feet of earth that covered her new, underground 'room'.

"Hello, Jeanette. What have you got there?" I asked.

"It's our Anderson shelter. Dad's only just finished putting it together. Did you want to come inside and have a look?"

"All right," I said, rather bemused by the strange little building buried in the ground.

The pair of us immediately – but carefully – entered the sub-surface structure. Jeanette led the way (although, with the building being only about six feet long, there was little chance of my actually getting lost!). I followed her, bending over so as not to hit my head on the low entrance.

The dark, dank form now covered and hid us both. Only a

limited amount of light came in through the small doorway, illuminating the grey structure. I sat down on the rudimentary floor and stretched out my arms to feel the space around me; the metal sides that I touched were cold and damp with condensation.

"Dad's going to put some bunks in it..." she said, pointing at the sides where they would go, "... and then we can all sleep in here."

I wondered why they suddenly had to sleep outside and underground, and then Jeanette somewhat clarified everything when she said that people like her were only going to be sleeping underground if a war was to come.

I stood up and wondered how high the roof was. I tried jumping with my arm held aloft; I almost hit my head on the curved side in the process.

"You look like you want to ask the teacher something," Jeanette quipped. "Mum's going to lay some flowers to make it look nicer outside. She said it was a bit sad to leave it looking so bare."

The whole construction was about six feet tall. Most of it was below the surface – like an iceberg would be, floating in the sea. It felt almost as though I was entombed within one; it gave me an uncomfortable chill.

End of naivety – reality takes over
"Does that word say Czechoslovakia?" I asked my mother, expectantly.

"That's right," she said.

It meant little to me in 1939. The name that I could barely pronounce, sat on the same front page of the newspaper as another, more familiar one – *Germany*.

Summer term 1939 came and I was given a letter from my teacher to pass to my parents. The letter originated from a committee of about three or four women who were sponsored by the government to work with the school. Their job was to ask the parents of the hundreds of children who went there, for permission to allow their children to be sent away to the quiet countryside in the event of a war breaking out. (The phrase 'quiet countryside' only applied, of course, to those regions of the country that were not yet billeting hundreds of children.)

Like so many others, my mother consented to her children leaving the country's great capital city, should war come. In such a time, it seemed as though there was to be no room at the centre of the metropolis, for the innocents. She was given a list of the things that I was to prepare to take in the event of my going away: a complete change of clothes and essential toiletries such as a toothbrush, soap, flannel and a comb. For meal-times at my new residence, I would need my own cutlery and a cup. It all seemed a lot for just a few days' absence and seemed to indicate a time away that was going to last several weeks, perhaps even longer. For the journey, I was advised to take some food such as sandwiches, biscuits and fruit.

When I asked my mother for how long I might be leaving her, she confidently told me not to worry about it and predicted, 'It'll never happen'. She then decided it would 'not be too long' if it did, which did little to put my mind at rest.

My mother had to do a little needlework on some of her children's clothes to bring them up to a presentable state. Afterwards, those and others that looked nearly as good as new, were carefully folded and kept safely to one side, to preserve them in case they were to be needed in the near future.

My mother began listening more frequently to the radio as the weeks went by and we seemed to be collecting more newspapers than usual. For us young ones, though, the only thing that concerned us was our latest school holiday and whether or not we were going to be able to fit all of our games into it. In the streets – the 'summer playground' for children like me – there was familiarity and, almost every day, a welcoming warm, bright, shining sun.

"Poland!" I heard my mother suddenly exclaim. "They've done it!"

Poland!

September 1939 arrived. The time for playing with my friends was coming to an abrupt end, to be replaced by a sense of inevitability, incomprehension, helplessness and foreboding, as the start of the new month heralded the sudden advance of the mighty, new German war machine into its smaller, innocent Polish neighbour. Apprehension began to pervade all thoughts except those of the youngest of children, who seemed enthralled somewhat by the possibility of momentous events taking over their otherwise insignificant lives.

"Are we at war?" I asked my mother.

"No. Not yet," she replied.

Distant, violent political events were now appearing to take hold of my family's ordered lives. When the British Government issued an ultimatum to Germany, my mother's mood in the house became noticeably more sombre. Her only remedy for it was just to keep sending her children outside to play or to make us all more cups of tea.

By the third of September, on the Sunday morning, my mother gathered her whole family around the radio in order to listen to an important announcement by the Prime Minister, Neville Chamberlain. We sat or stood quietly to hear the news. I could not help but feel that the occasion was not going to have a positive outcome.

While a part of me relished, in anticipation, the excitement at some of the changes that a war might bring, I could see from my mother's expressions and behaviour that I might not have much to look forward to if it was war. My mother no longer seemed able to do anything to alter what was happening to her family. She appeared powerless and sad and so vulnerable at the unwelcome approach of a menacing fate.

After a few minutes, the voice of the announcer declared that the Prime Minister was about to speak. It had just passed eleven o'clock, the time that we had earlier been told was the expiration of Great Britain's ultimatum to Germany.

Mr Chamberlain, sitting in the cabinet room of 10 Downing Street, began relaying to an expectant nation the futile last act, that morning, of the British ambassador in Berlin. With a heavy, laboured tone – which was ideal for preparing his audience for some particularly unpleasant news – Chamberlain sombrely declared, "... that no such undertaking has been received and that, consequently, this country is... at war... with Germany." He continued a little more, to speak of his personal struggle for peace, but he personified now only the image of a broken man, whose final act was just to shatter the insidious fantasy of his own creation – the venerated cruel illusion of 'peace in our time'.

Nancy and Doris were too young to understand the consequences of anything just uttered. Arthur immediately looked forward to some thrilling stories of battles involving our armed forces – forces that we were often told were the best in the world. Meanwhile, my mother sat quietly in her seat for a minute, apparently lost in her own thoughts. When she perked up a little, she asked us who would like a cup of tea.

For my part, I had emotions that were somewhere between all of those. I felt stalwart, outwardly confident and thoughtful, and if I felt a little naïve, then I was untroubled by it. Perhaps, without realising it, that was now the best way to be. Perhaps I was also not that different from the man on the radio to whom I had just been listening!

Within a matter of minutes, just after we had finished our calming drinks of tea, a dozen local air-raid sirens unexpectedly started to cry out their telling harmonies.

"Oh, God! It's starting!" my mother ejaculated.

She jumped up from her seat and instructed us all to get our gas masks without a moment's delay. After she had desperately grabbed her own, she ensured that all of her brood had theirs as well and were thus suitably equipped for surviving being poisoned by a gas cloud that she was imminently expecting.

Then she shepherded everyone quickly out of the room and down into the street, where the mechanical, undulating wailing of the alarms seemed louder and more urgent than ever. Ruefully they signalled the impending approach of indiscriminate death on a wing: a high, impersonal, industrial killing machine; the invisible terminator of civilisation; the final visitor of us all.

We left our home behind and scrambled along to our improvised shelter: the basement of the brewery, opposite our house, that we had previously been told we could use in an air raid. We rushed into the large, cold space and hastily sat down. At such a dangerous time, we children looked to our mother for courage and inspiration but that was perhaps the worst thing to do; she possibly looked the most worried of us all. Nancy started taking things quite badly... and we waited. Outside, we heard other families rushing around. The police – the managers of confusion, complacency, calm and panic, who had just started sporting their new, military-style helmets – directed and hurried the late, fleeing members of the local community into our basement or into other 'shelters' farther down the street.

After a few more people had joined us in our refuge, the two heavy doors were firmly closed and we were all just left to sit and await the coming storm. I was holding my gas mask, just as everyone else was doing with theirs, and wondered if we should be putting them on – just in case!

"Shouldn't we put our gas masks on?" I asked.

"If there was gas," my mother said, "they'd tell us. They've got rattles and you'd hear them cycling up and down rattling them if we were being gassed."

With that information, we all began listening for rattles, which became easier when the sirens ominously fell silent.

"What if they've broken their rattles... or they can't find them," Arthur thoughtfully but disquietingly interjected.

"They're careful with them. They won't break or lose them. They're too important," my mother replied, attempting to reassure us.

She did not allay my new fear, though. I was meant to assume the absence of gas until I heard otherwise but I was now worrying in case something had happened to the ARP people to stop them warning us, which would have left us all patiently sitting in our shelter and about to die of ignorance. I held my ever-more important gas mask box close to me... waiting to be gassed... and sniffed... carefully.

No bombs were dropping... so far. No drones of aircraft menaced the peace. As the minutes passed, it really had seemed that the fear of war was worse than the war itself. Patiently we carried on straining to listen for the first approach of aircraft, the explosions of bombs, and the rattle of the all-important gas warning.

Eventually, the authorities realised that they had been a little too quick to assume that it was the beginning of the end of their world. It had been a false alarm and the monotonic 'all clear' sang out from the sirens. The sound was higher-pitched, yet quieter, than the earlier *warning* calls had been. It let us know that the flighty danger had passed – at least for now.

My family – a little more tense than we had started the day – left the security of the shelter and made our way back home. There, we listened to more informative and rousing radio bulletins, and we partook of some more calming cups of tea. Later that day, my mother perked up a little when she heard King George's rallying speech on the radio.

Everyone felt less alone at that dark hour when our neighbours across the Channel – the powerful French nation – also declared war against Germany. The radio announced as well that the experienced war hero – the politician Mr Winston Churchill – had become the First Lord of the Admiralty, just as he had been during the Great War. My mother informed us that the Germans could not beat his ships in the conflict some twenty-odd years earlier and she confidently predicted that they were not going to do it this time either! She said that the Germans would never get past 'Winny's great battleships' (as she called them) and that we had nothing to worry about.

Everyone seemed to be taking comfort from all of our virtuous institutions that were now coming to the fore in the emerging struggle of good against evil. Now was the time for the failed guardians of the legacy of the *first* world war, to pass their wisdom and knowledge to the ingenious minds of a potential *second* world war – by whose services the latest impressive annihilation of humanity was certain to be conducted on a scale worthy of the inheritance. As we began entering a state of the unknown – where even staying alive another day seemed far less predictable than it did twenty-four hours earlier – my community discovered new strengths in its shared adversity.

"What will be, will be," my mother resignedly said that night, leaving the problems of another day down to fate. As she was losing control of her family to the vagaries of a time of unknown duration and severity, it was for the benefit – and subject to the wisdom – of the greater good and its immaculate purpose that she was finally surrendering her family.

3

Off to who knows where?

The knock at the door –
the lights were going out and so was I

EVERYONE IN THEIR homes now had to put up thick curtains in order to comply with the new 'black-out' regulations. They were to deny the attractive shafts of a betraying flickering evening light to an intruding German air force.

"Put that light out!" the local air-raid warden would uncompromisingly yell at anyone not complying with the government directive.

Within a couple of days of the war starting, a middle-aged woman, who was a volunteer from the committee/school partnership, came and was (unfortunately) reassured by my mother that she had not had a change of mind about sending her children away.

My mother was therefore informed that she was to prepare her children for an evacuation that was to take place in two days. We children were to go to our school early on that prescribed morning and take with us all of our belongings that we would need during our absence, in something like a suitcase or haversack – or even a pillowcase if we did not have anything else. She may have felt encouraged to suggest the last option after a glance from the doorway at the unfortunate circumstances in which we lived.

The long goodbye

On the morning of the evacuation, my mother woke me early. Although I was aware of some aspects of the war that had just started, the purpose, manner and final result of an evacuation still remained vague. I wondered where I was going, and why. Being ten years of age, I could not comprehend everything that was happening to me but I knew that my free and happy life as a London girl was about to end. Panic set in. What about my friends, who I had expected would always be with me, I asked myself. The safe routine of my life was about to be altered; I feared for the uncertain future.

After finishing breakfast – which seemed to require more than the usual effort – I went into the kitchen, poured the pot of hot water on the gas stove into the large, round wash-bowl in the sink, and proceeded to clean myself... slowly.

"Come on Lily, don't take too long or you and Doris will be late," my mother called out after a few minutes.

Doris was going to use the kitchen after me and then she joined in as well with: "Come on Lily, I've got to get washed too!"

With resistance proving futile, I sped up, cleaned my teeth and forlornly vacated the room, moving that one step closer to my evacuation as I did so.

After dressing, I finished the packing of my possessions, which included spare handkerchiefs (young children with sniffles can probably never have too many handkerchiefs), some stationery for the ubiquitous school-work that apparently was to follow me wherever I went, and my one luxury – my old rag doll. It was rather worn but because it was also small and light, it was easy to carry. It would be my comfort, reminding me of the happy times at home that, I felt, were soon to be left far behind. My indispensable, boxed gas mask crowned the final assemblage, sitting as it did on the top.

After last-minute dashes to the kitchen to quench our dry throats with a refreshing drink of water, Doris, Arthur and I re-collected our assigned packages and went through the front door that was being held open for us by our stoical, overseeing matriarch. I noticed how firmly it seemed to be closed behind us.

The early morning air was cool and bracing as we three small children were urged along like ducklings led by their anxious mother duck. Soon enough, we approached the school – our place of departure – and found its gates completely obscured by the mass of mothers and a few fathers who had arrived before us. They and their children, like me, generally seemed to be in smart apparel, which was quite an unusual sight for our neighbourhood. It was almost as though they were trying to tell the school something of their families that their poverty had previously kept hidden.

I overheard the advice that some of the parents were giving their young ones, words of great meaning – the ways that their children should conduct themselves in the future – spoken as though they were the cardinal thoughts to last a lifetime. When their children passed beyond the imposing entrance, many of the adults behaved as though these were the last occasions that their children were to be with them; the mass of general melancholy presented an appropriate image of heartbroken love, a proud picture of emotions that their little boys and girls could remember them by. Tears were not entirely absent from the scene – from either side of the hard, dividing gates.

Now it was our turn. Our mother ensured that we were carrying our bags and that our coats were done up. She tidied my hair and looked at me for a moment, and then attended to Doris. She then did likewise to Arthur. From her pocket, she took out a small handful of change and gave each of us a shilling and a few pennies.

Poor Doris thought that my mother was going to be

evacuated as well. She was soon enlightened that only I and possibly Arthur were going to be staying with her but that – as previously arranged – I would always be looking after her. This seemed to somewhat placate Doris and she noticeably cheered up in a direct proportion to the amount that I suddenly became more depressed.

"Do what the teachers tell you," we were all told, "And Doris… stay with Lily at all times."

"Yes, mum," she replied.

"And Lily… you're looking after Doris, all right?" mother added.

"I know," I dutifully replied and, with that, she kissed each of us on the cheek.

As we all said our goodbyes, we passed through to the other side of the gates, to be with the rest of the children. Although I so disliked my immediate circumstances that my mother's actions had put me into, I was mature enough to realise that there was a benevolent purpose behind them. Her attitude to the events of recent days had been stalwart throughout and I somehow knew that I had to deal with the unknown situation developing before me – accepting what fate had in store for me – in the same confident manner. I was beginning to understand her motives and methods better and suddenly felt older for it. As I stood less afraid to face the trials of an imminent uncertain, life-changing future, I was aware that I was becoming better prepared for it, emotionally.

Arthur quickly found some of his school friends and went over to them but I stayed with Doris, who held my hand tightly; this was all a new experience for her at this school and she was still a little nervous.

After about quarter of an hour, a teacher appeared at the entrance of the school building. She rang a bell that she was carrying and instructed us to all get into our year groups and then go into the school. I told Doris to go as directed – with the group of similarly aged youngsters – and that I would see her later.

Some children were absent from my classroom, so – presumably – those children's parents did not have the same resolve as my mother had to evacuate all of her children. It seemed too early to judge as to who was making the right decision.

The teacher took a bunch of brown luggage labels from her desk. Then, as each of our names was called from the class register, those who were present went up to her, whereupon she tied one of the labels to our clothing. Each label contained that child's name and home address, as well as one or two reference numbers, which identified our particular school.

As we were being labelled, we were asked if our parents had given us a stamped, addressed postcard to send home from our eventual destination. Those without such a postcard, such as me, were given one from the teacher. None of the people in the class at that time knew where we were going, so the address – to where any replies from our parents could be sent – was left blank.

We were next asked if we all had the necessary things that we were supposed to be taking. Everyone said yes but I do not think that the teacher could have done much anyway, even if we had not. For instance, she obviously had no ready supply of complete changes of clothes for all of her twenty-odd children, if we had required them.

Specially prepared fruit and sandwiches were given to those who were not so provisioned, with the remaining food being divided equally among the class so that we all ended up having a second little breakfast!

The atmosphere in my old classroom was unusual, almost surreal. My fellow pupils were unsurprisingly subdued but my cold, authoritarian teacher had changed the most. She was mellower, like a caring nurse; almost like a mother, perhaps.

Visits to the toilet were encouraged, while the opportunity remained. A woman entered the classroom, to be told that we were ready to leave. She then nodded and left. We all looked around at each other. Nothing else was said, so I returned to resting my tired head back down in my arms on my desk.

After about another ten minutes, the school bell tolled. We returned to the playground, to be lined up and counted. With us were the teachers and – to assist with the evacuation, and identifiable by their white armbands – some volunteer adults. They were mostly women and possibly the mothers of some of the children being evacuated. Their times to say their goodbyes were still to come. When all of the preparations were complete, the headmistress hesitated as though savouring the moment – the sight of her cherished school as it was, possibly for the last time.

Suddenly, she cried out the order: "Off we go then!"

The gates were re-opened. Then, in neat lines – at least to start with – my almost complete school followed the volunteers and teachers who went ahead to part the sea of parents.

We marched down the road closely shadowed by the parents, who appeared ready to pounce on any stragglers. I felt that if any of us children were to fall behind, we would be held by the mob of love, smothered with affection and never again released. They never stopped watching us as we were being taken away from them. They never fell too far behind, while the volunteers never let them get too close. The headmistress determinedly drove the procession on. Always mindful of the stalking pack behind us, she never allowed the pace to drop.

As we went, we actually neared my house, and I imagined for a moment that I was returning because it had all been some sort of dreadful mistake... 'Sorry, Lilian. The war's been cancelled. You can go home again now.'

However, we passed my house without hesitating and

continued into the next road… and the next. Then the railway station – a great cathedral-like structure – appeared. My modest school, now only one of many, was shepherded into the concourse with an air of expectation as though off on some kind of adventure of a lifetime. Some impatient souls began making 'choo-choo' sounds like a railway engine, in their eagerness to feel that they had already begun their trip on a steam train, possibly the first in their lives. Against a wall, a nurse – who appeared to have been drafted in specially for the occasion – was attending to a distressed, and probably homesick, young girl. Nearby, a boy stood rubbing his red, sore hands, which had become that way after all of his gripping of his bag's rough string handles. Beyond the cacophony of a jumbled mass of a thousand wayfarers, were the parents, remaining outside, waving once more and calling out their ineffectual goodbyes, for a last time.

When I saw Doris some distance away, I managed to force my way through the bustling throng to her and hold her small hand. It immediately grasped mine tightly as though, if her strength weakened, we might part once more in the maelstrom and never meet again. She was not happy and I almost felt that I wanted to cry myself but I did not wish to add to her worries by letting her think that even the person looking after her, was losing control!

Suddenly, a teacher ushered us along with the rest of the children to the platform. Beside it, a very long train was waiting for us. It welcomed its passengers with a huff and a puff, and seemed almost as tired before the start of its journey as *we* were!

"Where are we going to, Miss?" someone asked a teacher but 'out to the country' was the only response that we were ever to hear.

The volunteers shepherded us waifs aboard a relatively unoccupied carriage. However, the situation descended rapidly towards pandemonium when thirty or so other children piled in just as we sat down! Neatly ironed and folded clothes fell out of makeshift suitcases before being retrieved and carelessly squashed back inside. The food that fell out of bags was trodden on, wiped 'clean' and later often cunningly swapped for someone else's clean food. There was screaming and shouting as arguments ensued as to who was going to sit on the outside ("… seats, nearest the windows," that is, not "… of the carriage").

While the last of the children, volunteers and teachers were entering the carriages, the engine readied itself with more huffing and puffing, and as the children all around me started shouting and cheering even louder, the train accompanied the chorus with its own hissing vents of steam. I moved towards the open window and found myself joining in with the clamour.

Whistles came from the platform and hoots of reply flew from the engine. Then, with the screeching of metal wheels slipping on their metal tracks and a jolt as they finally gripped them, the first train journey taken by most, if not all, of us hundreds of evacuees began, simultaneously accompanied by our uniform and boisterous crescendo of approval.

To the country

We moved along slowly at first, as though respectfully observing the passing of a way of life. Tall, grey, soot-encrusted buildings went by. Lines of flapping, drying washing 'waved farewell'. Factory chimneys, from a world of industry, smoked nonchalantly; they paid no attention to us at all.

As though we were seeing London for the first time, we fought for viewing space at the crowded, open windows. The city gave way to suburbia. Buildings were no longer crammed together or forced to fight for space as they had been in London. The view of close, communal living and dark-grey, soot-covered buildings became one of more open spaces and occasional light-grey, partially soot-covered buildings. We stopped at the odd station and picked up a few more people but no more evacuees.

Suddenly, someone exclaimed, "Look! Fields!"

Then someone else asked, "Where are the cows, then?"

As we travelled on, coloured splotches on the horizon came nearer and became the first farm animals that I had ever seen in the flesh. They were *cows*!

I cried, "They're cows!" and those around me looked at them in awe. I looked for Doris and managed to get her to the window, to have a good look as well.

"Look at that, Doris..." I said, "... and they're eating the grass."

All the children in the carriage looked out as well and saw that, truly, the cows *were* eating the grass.

And so this force of London children identified more examples of country life – cows, sheep, horses and farmers farming, and still farther we moved, deeper into strange, unknown lands. On we trundled.

About an hour into our trip, we approached a station and

screeched to a halt. We looked anxiously at the evacuation volunteer who had been in our carriage since the start of the journey, whose duties included ensuring that we were only to get off at the right station. This time, people on the platform gave the command, for everyone to exit their carriages. Out we staggered, quite tired and thirsty. What were we doing there, I had to ask myself. The wisdom behind the day's prolonged journey still somewhat eluded me. Little made sense any more.

Then onto buses to the school hall

The volunteers with us said their goodbyes and remained behind, while the teachers and we children were shepherded outside the station and onto several waiting buses. We drove for some ten minutes to a school that had been opened specially for the occasion.

In the hall, we joined the many children who had just arrived before us. Behind tables of free buns and rolls were women who were busily pouring and distributing lovely hot, refreshing mugs of tea to the mass of weary travellers.

Time to be chosen

As Doris and I sat quietly enjoying our welcome nourishment, my attention was drawn to the many adults who were walking around and scrutinizing us evacuees as though preparing to purchase an animal or 'goods' from a shop. When they neared, they usually showed little politeness; words such as 'Hello', 'Please' or 'Goodbye' rarely passed their lips.

After each cursory examination, the adults began looking at the next unfortunate soul. It was a time to watch and to *be* watched; it was strange and unnerving. Things became clearer when an official made a welcoming speech to those assembled, explaining that while the country was in its troubled times of conflict, his local community had opened up their hearts and homes to offer each of us evacuees a place of retreat. The people walking around and examining us were, he explained, 'the kind ones' who were going to be offering the sanctuary.

As Doris and I were therefore among the hundreds who were now to be given a place to stay by someone of 'good will', I quickly decided that the next few minutes were going to be vital, if we were going to manage to acquire for ourselves a home away from home. I told Doris that if someone came up to us whom we liked the look of, we were to be on our best behaviour. Unfortunately, as the minutes passed, there were not that many people whom we *did* like the look of and – worse still – there were not that many who seemed all that interested in us, either!

When I told any inquiring adults that we were sisters and that I was told to stay with Doris, most potential benefactors became uninterested in us; they wanted just the one or the other of us but not a matching pair. People apparently could – and did – pick evacuees who were most suited to their circumstances, requirements and tastes. What we evacuees wanted, seemed to count for little.

Big, strong-looking boys were being selected, probably for a lot of hard work later. Meanwhile, individual elegant, cute little girls were having their hair stroked and their head patted; they were possibly to play the part of the new family 'pet'. That they were not given a big ball of wool to play with while their hosts were busy completing the necessary paperwork, seemed something of an oversight.

A child appearing precocious would often be chosen to join the kind of family that could afford the luxury of a motor car. At the other extreme, a lot of distressed and rough-looking children – made even less presentable after the recent long and gruelling journey – despite possibly being of good character, were to be damned and made to feel so by their outward display of misfortune. Little was done to improve the impression of themselves that they were giving to the outsiders. Some of the hosts walking around seemed rather shocked by those children's appearances and stayed clear of them.

Of the many teachers who had kindly – or compulsorily – accompanied us to this part of the country, few appeared to be offered places to stay. As a group, they appeared the most unwanted of all. For the first time, I felt sorry for them too. I thought that adults would have preferred the company of other adults but the circling hosts seemed to be choosing the children first.

Perhaps the young were thought to be less trouble, easier to please and less complaining. There was interesting sociological behaviour afoot. [The phrase 'interesting sociological behaviour' did not immediately occur to me (although I knew what 'afoot' was) but I had plenty of time to witness its unpleasant manifestations and consider its causes and the need for good, big words to describe it.]

About an hour after arriving in the hall, I noticed the official was looking at us with a rather disappointed expression. Fearing the accommodation that anyone left unchosen might be forced to accept, I decided that Doris and I had to try harder – somehow – to get ourselves picked. We tidied ourselves up a bit. Poor Doris attended to her hair as best as she could; I helped her. Then we tried smiling at every prospective good foster parent but our hearts were really not in it any more – although they were not really in it all that much to start with!

After a while, a rather plump, middle-aged woman and an athletic man who appeared to be in his early twenties and looked like Tyrone Power (although he was not the famous actor, unfortunately) approached and asked us our names.

"Lilian, Miss," I said, almost enthusiastically.

"Doris, Miss," added my tired sister.

They looked at us for a while. The woman lifted our

chins for a moment to have a good look at our faces. We stared back at her.

"Care to come and live on our farm with us?" she asked (after having first put our chins down again).

Aware that we might get no better offer if we refused, and that Doris and I would now at least be able to stay together, we humbly accepted the invitation and prayed as best as we could that whatever we were about to receive, we were both going to be truly grateful!

"Come along with me then, you two," she said and we followed our new 'foster parents' to the official who had been closely watching us earlier.

"I'll take these two," the woman said happily, as though she had just luckily obtained some sort of 'two-for-the-price -of-one' bargain!

The official looked down at us. I smiled a little with satisfaction, betraying my relief that we were not going to be the most unwanted children in the hall.

The woman gave her name to the man, who examined our labels and wrote our names on a form that he was holding. He then asked for the postcards that Doris and I had earlier received. After we handed them to him, he wrote our new billet address on them and returned them to us. He told us to write a message on them for our mother and post them to her as soon as we could, to let her know where we had gone and that we were well.

The woman then instructed us to stand beside the nearby wall: "Now then, you two, you're mine, so I want you to stand over there and don't let anyone else take you."

She then returned to her travels around the room, to obtain some more 'waifs' to add to her collection. When four boys and one other girl had finally been acquired, the man and woman led us all outside to a line of vehicles, at the end of which was an old truck.

"You two young 'uns, inside with me," she said, directing

Doris and the other girl into one side of the cabin while she got into the driver's seat on the other side.

After everyone's luggage was placed on the back of the truck, it went ahead to the farm, leaving the other four boys and me to follow the young man there on foot. When one of the boys asked how far away the farm was, the man replied that it was fifty miles and that we would have to run all of the way there if we were to make it before nightfall! Seeing himself surrounded by five waifs, who were looking very rough and on the verge of revolting, he corrected himself and apologised, saying that it was only about three miles away. He said that we were fortunate because he knew a quick way and that it should therefore *only* take us about an hour or so to get there.

After our early evening route-march over holes, lumps and slippery stiles, and across short cuts of 'fields of wounds', we stopped momentarily when the man suddenly announced, "That's it."

"Hooray!" shouted a couple of the boys at our new home sitting peacefully in the distance.

I did not join in heartily; I had long since lost my spirit of adventure and, because of a dry throat, some of my voice as well. By now, I just wanted to get indoors, sit down, partake of the food and drink that I hoped would be waiting for me, and then go straight to bed.

Perhaps when I was to wake up the next morning, I thought, I would find myself in my old bed again, back in London, and this day would be remembered as just some very realistic, very bad dream. Perhaps all would be as it was yesterday. Perhaps... probably not... but for a moment at least, I could dream.

Our new home
We approached the farmhouse. Built of stone hundreds of years before, it had a fifteen-foot chimney of brick and more

stone, and a decades-old patched-up, mossy, low thatched roof. About half a dozen small windows ran along the length of the building, while more stone blocks filled in a similar number of window-sized areas.

A tall, lifeless tree firmly stood sentry at one end of the farmhouse, while a pile of old wooden containers decorated the other. The unfamiliar noises of farm animals contributed towards it being a very eerie, strange place. Several puddles concentrated everyone's tired minds; we avoided them as best we could. I could not see the bottom of any and I certainly did not want to fall and possibly sink up to my neck in one and then immediately need a bath the moment I arrived.

The sounds of a conversation emanated from inside the building. A dull light escaped through gaps in curtains that barely covered the windows. The man knocked on the door, which was shortly opened for us by the farm-woman, who welcomed us and bade us to go inside, which we did – all slowly, in a line, one slightly apprehensive child behind the other.

Immediately we were greeted by a gorgeous smell of freshly baked bread and some sort of stew. Then our nerves gripped us all again, when a strange noise came from the next room. It was almost as though someone was about to jump out from around the corner and frighten the life out of us. We waited for a few moments but when no one did come out and attack us, we began to settle down and relax. Just then, a large, black and white sheepdog came rushing up from the next room and almost bowled us all over!

"That's Bobby," said the man, who tried to calm the exuberant animal. Bobby was at least jumping up on us as an expression of instant affection rather than rabid aggression. He was almost playing a kind of strange 'Guess the Weight' game with each of us, whereby he would launch his entire beefy torso repeatedly upon our small, prostrate and defenceless bodies and then expect us to guess how long he was going to wait there. He was a friendly dog and he soon calmed down to the point where we were able to stroke him and get our faces and hands licked when we wanted them to be.

"Did you want something to eat or did you wanna keep playing with Bobby?" the man genuinely enquired.

We all said 'Eat!' – even the boy under the dog. So everyone not subject to canine restraint followed the man into the kitchen, where we all sat down on simple wooden chairs, each behind a bowl – none of which matched any other – set around a heavy, old dining table, and consumed some home-made bread and butter and a lovely steaming rabbit stew.

The rabbits had trespassed onto the farm and had been caught in one of the many snares – wire loops – that had been laid along the hedgerows, which was where the animals were most liable to be happily bouncing along. If the rabbits were not careful, they would get their necks caught in the wire and, in their hopeless struggles, they would dispatch themselves.

"Waste not, want not," said the pragmatic man of nature, happy to utilise the produce of the land whatever it was, wherever it came from and however fluffy, cuddly and attractively playful it might have been to start with.

"Come in when you're ready to meet us proper," the man said as he put his empty bowl and plate in the sink and went into the lounge.

With our meals finished, the other boys and I followed him.

"Come on in. We're not goin' to eat you," the woman promised as she pointed at the space on the floor where we children could sit. We entered the room through the doorway that supported a heavy oak door, and squatted where we were directed.

A middle-aged man sat one side of the woman. By her other side, sat the young man we had already met. All three reclined on large, comfortable-looking chairs – two of which matched.

In the middle of the wall facing the doorway, was a blazing log fire with a substantial surround of light and dark stone. Above it, attached to a wooden board, was a shiny horseshoe. To the right, a hundred or more wooden logs were piled five feet high, ready for the fire. Several large, black-painted oak beams supported the lounge's low ceiling, from which a basic chandelier was hanging. The modest illumination that came from the many candles that it held, supplemented the fire's enchanting glow.

Hanging up on the wall at the side was a deer's head. It had a bowler hat on one of its two antlers and a Panama on the other; the back of it was adorned with a huntsman's riding cap. A silver-framed mirror was next to the head. For the window that was beside it – and in several other places around the building – wooden shutters were used in place of curtains.

On the opposite wall, there were three paintings. One was of a young man whose appearance seemed very dated; one appeared to be some sort of family group; and the other was of a country scene in summer, of rolling green and yellow hills, distant hedgerows and thick borders of tall trees. In front of us children was a long, polished wooden table; and in front of that, were our hosts – looking down on us from their comfortable vantage points.

"Are you all getting to know each other now, then?" the woman asked.

No, I thought. "Yes," I said, like everyone else on the floor.

"So, who are you all, again?" she asked.

"Bernard, Miss," said one boy.

"Roger, Miss," said another.

"Lilian, Miss," said I.

"Alexander, Miss," said the third boy.

"Martin, Miss," said the last and eldest-looking boy.

The woman looked and smiled at us and we all smiled back at her in that laboured air of congeniality.

"Don't call me 'Miss'. I've not been a 'Miss' for a long time," she explained in a light-hearted way, as though she was now missing the carefree single days of her distant youth. "'Ere's why," she said, pointing at the man to her left. "'E's my 'usband, Mr Greenwood."

"You can call me… Mr Greenwood," he explained, after a pause. He had a large physique, probably from a lifetime of hard manual farm labour. In fact, his whole family seemed perfectly suited to the demanding environment in which they were surviving, as though the very fabric of it was in their blood, and had been so for many generations.

"So you can all call me Mrs Greenwood. All right? And you've met my son, Daniel, of course," she prompted, pointing at the young man on a chair to her right, of whose company we had just had the pleasure.

"Yes, Miss," we said, although Daniel had never bothered to introduce himself formerly, even when he was getting us to traipse all over the countryside on the way to his farm.

"Where are you all from?" Daniel asked.

We all said that we were from London. In the process, Roger and Alexander disclosed that they were brothers.

"And are you staying here for the whole war?" Daniel asked.

My stomach suddenly turned as I contemplated such a horrible eventuality. Martin, by contrast, apparently had no worries of that kind.

"I should be leaving school next year," he confidently said, "So I suppose I'll be going home and then out to work."

"I don't know," I said, when the adults looked at me. It was all a strange question-and-answer session. I felt nervous at the occasional interjected silences.

"Anyway, we shouldn't be talking about leaving when

you've only just arrived," Mrs Greenwood said, adding, "We can see about showing you the animals tomorrow. You'd like that, wouldn't you?"

"Oh, yes," said a couple of the boys, their enthusiasm contrasting markedly with the ambivalence that I now felt towards the livestock.

"I can see you noticed that," Mr Greenwood said to Alexander, who had been staring at a model of a wooden wagon and horses that was displayed on a shelf. "I made that. Carved it, I did, out of oak... a couple of winters' ago. I'll take it down and show it to you tomorrow, if you like."

"'E gets the wood from the old tree out there," Daniel said, pointing at the farmland outside (appropriately).

"It's 'is 'obby," added Mrs Greenwood. "'E's done loads, carved lots of lovely models all round the place, all out of that oak tree. Does it in the evenings."

The end of a long day
At that late hour, with the small talk getting ever smaller, I found myself growing tired. My heavy eyelids were losing their noble struggle against gravity and my waning will was surrendering to the sullen singularity of the new surroundings. Fortunately, we were soon advised to go to bed, as there was nothing to stay up for and we would benefit from a good night's sleep after such a long and hectic day. Mr Greenwood disquietingly added, though, that they tended to start work on the farm very early in the morning. He also said that the cockerels would probably be waking us up as well, when they would start their crowing at daybreak – or even earlier, at about four in the morning, if the moon was visible! So, just when I had been eagerly looking forward to a nice recuperative period of rest, I now – regrettably – could anticipate so little.

We were taken through the farmhouse and shown the outside toilet, to which we could risk trying to find our way in the middle of the night. If we did not wish to attempt such a long and hazardous journey, we had to use the chamber-pots instead, which were in our bedrooms. As we had only just arrived and we had not yet got used to the environment, we were advised that there would probably be the least likelihood of an accident at night if we just used the pots for the time being. I was disappointed to discover that my initial experiences of an evacuation were to have so much in common with those of my younger years.

All of us children then picked up our own suitcases and bags, which had earlier been piled in the corner of the lounge, and proceeded to follow Mrs Greenwood through the dimly lit property. On the way, we passed an alcove with a semi-circular window at the back of it and a curious display in front, consisting of a long table covered in half a dozen bunches of flowers, a full-sized wagon wheel and – resting on a wooden frame above the table – a saddle. Above all of that, hanging on the wall at the back of the assemblage, was a substantial-looking shotgun. Lying on the floor, underneath the table, was a length of thick rope.

We all continued along and up some narrow stairs, at the top of which was a painting with a simple wooden frame, of someone in a stable who was attending to the hooves of a horse. We slowed a little as we passed it, and then carried on to the end of the tiny corridor. We stopped outside a small room that was furnished with a couple of bunk beds.

"That's yours," Mrs Greenwood said, directing the boys to their beds and chests of drawers, before leaving them to unpack and go to bed.

Mrs Greenwood then took me back along the other way down the corridor, to where I was reintroduced to my sister and Geraldine (the other girl whom I had met earlier), who were in the girls' room.

"Hello, Lily," Doris delightfully said, obviously very pleased to be reunited with her sister.

"Hello, Doris," I replied, equally delighted to be seeing her again.

Mrs Greenwood showed me a chest of drawers for my use and left me to unpack and sort my possessions into it. She did not leave us a candle, as it was a bit too dangerous while we were still so disorganised. We were told to leave our curtains open and use the twilight instead, until we had finished changing and were ready to get into our beds.

Before I got into bed, I went over to the small window to look outside. When Geraldine and Doris saw me gazing out, they sat up and looked as well, from their high top-bunk positions.

Below me were several farm buildings with brown brick walls and grey roofs. The one nearest to me had skylights every few feet. I was able to make out what appeared to be the stable; and another was more like a simple shelter, being only a long roof that was held up by tall, thin supports – it had no walls.

All of these buildings sat around a large open yard, and beyond them, stretching as far as I could see, were fields laid with carpets of yellow, green and brown crops. With the setting sun, their colours were fading fast to grey. They lay still, except for the occasional ripple caused by a passing evening breeze. A few clumps of trees were scattered here and there. The view was very picturesque, framed as it was by extensive high, green hedgerows.

In that air of encouraging calm, I tried reflecting positively upon the day's events. That I should become pragmatic about my situation and learn from my experiences – good or bad – seemed to make the most sense. Just then, Doris interrupted my thoughts.

"Lily?" she said.

"Yes?"

"I want to go home," she sighed.

"So do I," I replied.

I immediately felt worse for not knowing when, if ever, we would be returning home. Nevertheless, I had let her know that she was not alone in her feelings of dejection.

"Me, too," interjected Geraldine. Now we all, in that small room, wanted to go home and we all knew it – for whatever good that was.

As I returned to my bed and sat down on it, I was very conscious of being in a room with two other very homesick girls. I was not feeling much better than they were but I reminded myself that at least I had managed to bring Doris with me without a serious incident, we had found somewhere relatively comfortable to stay and our hosts – the Greenwoods – seemed friendly enough. We children had not managed too badly so far, I thought. We had made a good start.

It had been a long day and I had gone through the whole panoply of emotions: confusion, fear, abandonment, excitement, nerves, rejection, acceptance, nausea, tiredness and redemption. I had much to think of, and recover from, soon, in the Freudian 'couch' of my dreams.

4

Lilian and Doris go a farmin'

Doin' the cows

EARLY THE NEXT morning, Mrs Greenwood came in and woke the other girls and me from a much-needed and refreshing good night's sleep. She put a towel and a tin bowl on the small table at the side of the room and left a large jug of warm water beside it.

"That's for you all to wash in," she instructed.

I realised straight away that only one of us at a time was meant to use it and then – obviously – only for our faces. If we needed a bath at any time, it was available in a small room, next to the kitchen.

At present, we were told that if we needed any more water, we had to go downstairs with the jug and get it ourselves.

"When you've finished with it, just toss it out of the window," she said.

We looked at the bowl... then the window... and then Mrs Greenwood.

"You toss the *water* out of the window, girls, not the bowl," she emphasised. "Bring down your crockery and cutlery, if you've got any," she said, before she left us.

At the start of my first complete day away from home, I was more at ease than I was the previous day. I had found out where I was now living – near Spalding, in Lincolnshire – and my only worry was about what the coming day would bring.

We went downstairs and had a cup of tea and small bowl of

porridge each. The other options for breakfast were a couple of slices of bread and butter – with something other than just butter between them if we were lucky – toast or something created through Mrs Greenwood's sense of imaginative improvisation!

After breakfast, Mrs Greenwood took everyone down to the cowshed, to show us the cows 'being done'. At the entrance of the large, noisy building, I noticed a grated drain cover, which allowed any filth emanating from the cows in the shed, to pass into the drain. From there, it would travel down to the giant cesspit, which was, understandably, some distance from the farm buildings.

Apparently, because the drain was positioned by the opening of the shed, the cows would wipe their feet on it on their way back out, after milking, thereby possibly sending more filth to the cesspit. I assumed that the wiping of the cows' feet, as described by the farmer, just happened naturally as the cows walked over the drain and that it was not part of a polite bovine ritual to which I was never to be a witness... *"'Scuse me... Just wiping me trotters... Moo."*

Inside the building, Mr Greenwood, his son and two other men were all busily milking cows. There were four of them, all in a line, from a total herd of about twelve. All of the men were squeezing them in order to make their milk come out. That is, each man was working on his own cow and was squeezing the teats of it – the men were not trying to get the milk out of all of the cows at the same time, by squashing them all together...

"Heave!"

Each cow stood nonchalantly within its own semi-caged area, which – presumably – was to prevent it moving about too much while it was being milked. It was surprising to see the laborious efforts required in order to obtain the small squirts of milk that were coming out, but I was assured that the quantities soon mounted up.

Several milk churns were at the side of the milking area. Some were silver coloured; the rest, brown. At the far end of the shed, there was a separate small enclosure with straw laid down, where any calves that were poorly could be better accommodated. For the time being, fortunately, it was empty.

Mr Greenwood invited each of us to have a go at milking a cow. Roger, being the first to the stool beside the cow, then sat upon it (the stool, that is, not the cow).

"That's the way. Grab the udder," Mr Greenwood instructed.

Other *what*, I wondered. At that time, I did not know what an 'udder' was.

Roger was shown how to squeeze each teat, initially using his thumb and the next two fingers, followed by the rest of his hand. When the milk did start to come out and he could confidently repeat the actions, he was left to carry on doing it merrily by himself for a few minutes. Eventually, the cow was emptied and led outside, and a full one was brought in to be milked.

After a while, the girls and I started to get a little bored with watching the cows having their milk squeezed out of them, so we asked, and were allowed, to play in the empty field just outside.

Into a field!
Shouting wildly, we raced erratically towards one end of the wide, empty field of soft, green grass. A couple of hundred yards into our most liberating experience, Geraldine shrieked and suddenly stopped in her tracks.

"What have you done?" I enquired.

"What is it?" Doris asked.

"I think it's a poo!" Geraldine replied.

Doris and I raced across to her, where we beheld, by her feet, the largest poo that certainly I had ever seen.

"Is it a poo?" Geraldine asked, looking up at me as though I was some sort of distinguished authority on intestinal discharges.

"It's definitely a poo," I said, unfortunately reinforcing Geraldine's belief that I should be consulted on all such matters. When we saw more coiled excretions around us, we decided that they were not going to spoil our day's enjoyment and that we were just going to have to be a lot more careful where we put our feet in future!

As we made our way around the field, we chased away a sheep that was grazing quite close to our fence, and some 'shifty-looking' birds – as Geraldine put it – that had been busily pecking at something in the grass.

As the feathered fiends took to the sky, I warned them not to come back, adding, "That's it. Go and play down your own street... go on!"

After we had finished exhausting ourselves, we found an area of clean grass and collapsed upon it. While we lay huffing and puffing and getting our breath back, I noticed high above us large birds that were following imaginary circles in the bright blueness. Perhaps they were vultures, I wondered, ready to swoop down to start greedily feasting upon our fresh flesh, believing that we had just dropped dead after all of our energetic endeavours. We were certainly not moving very much, so we could definitely have given them the impression, from a distance, that we were now ready for eating. I decided to wiggle my feet a bit, to let them know that I still had some life left in me yet.

"They're not going to take me," I defiantly declared.

"Who's not going to take you?" Geraldine inquired.

"Take you where?" added Doris.

"Those," I said, pointing up at the hovering birds. "Those vultures... up there in the sky."

"Are they vultures?" Doris asked.

"They might be..." I paused momentarily, before adding: "... and if they get you, they'll eat you!"

I wanted to let her know how serious I imagined our situation was becoming.

"Oh," Doris replied in a matter-of-fact way and not exactly getting into the spirit of the immediate life-or-death thing.

I remained defiant. "If I'm going down, I'm going to go down fighting!"

"But you're already down," Geraldine pointed out. "You'll have to stand up first if you want to go down fighting," she so perceptively added.

"Well, I'm still going to fight them, anyway..." I declared, "... up *or* down. Come on then! Come and get me if you want a piece of me!" I bravely challenged the birds as I waved my clenched fists up at them.

"Perhaps you should let them know what they're getting. Show them a leg or something. That might bring them down," suggested Doris.

"Or send them away," added Geraldine.

"All right then," I said and so I stuck my leg up in the air and slowly waved it around for a bit.

"Perhaps they prefer eating feet first," Geraldine suggested, so I began waving my foot around a lot as well, while still keeping my leg in the air.

"You've still got your shoe and sock on, Lily. Perhaps they don't want their food all wrapped up. They want to see what you've got to offer," Doris said.

So I took my shoe and sock off and then waved my foot around but still the birds remained up high. Then Doris and Geraldine, believing that they might be the ones whom the birds wanted to feast upon, did the same with their feet; they waved them in the air as well but the birds continued to ignore us.

"What's wrong with our feet, then? Are they not good enough for you; is that it?" Geraldine shouted, as though upset that the birds did not even want to try to eat us!

Whatever the birds were considering for a meal that morning, it soon appeared not to include us.

"They're flying away now," I said, rather disappointedly.

"Go on, clear off!" Doris shouted up at our unwelcome visitors.

"Go and eat somebody else then! Go on!" added Geraldine, feigning anger and shaking her small, clenched, outstretched fist up in the air at them.

We thought that the decision of those birds – to fly away – was probably a wise one on their part, for we all heartily expressed how we would have fought off the terrible flying carnivores had they dared to come down for a bit of a nibble – foot-based or otherwise. (When I describe them as 'terrible flying carnivores', I mean that they appeared as terrible carnivores that were flying, not that they were carnivores that could not fly properly and kept bashing into each other.) We all put our socks and shoes back on and then went back to relaxing again.

In that period of calm, I spent some time discovering a little more about Geraldine. She was eight years old, with no brothers or sisters, and when she was evacuated with her school, she lost contact with everyone whom she knew. Her anxieties about ending up being billeted alone had come true in a sense and were such that they put Doris' and mine far more into perspective.

I had Doris to look after and I could not afford to start worrying about every lonely evacuee girl who was younger than I was. However, she was just the one pleasant Geraldine and she seemed eager only for some companionship and a sense, once more, of belonging. I could not be distant towards her... and neither did I want to be. Just as it could be said that there is safety in numbers, so I found myself feeling more secure by being with two companions – Geraldine and Doris – than I did, the day before, with just the one. Our fraternity – formed from shared insecurities caused by common adverse circumstances – was a comforting bond that I felt, and hoped, would give us the strength to face the trials of an uncertain future.

Pigs

After returning to the farmhouse for a refreshing drink of lovely cold water, Mrs Greenwood took us to feed the pigs. We carried to the pigsty a couple of heavy buckets of unwanted food – potato peelings, old cabbage leaves and similar items of matter that were considered unsuitable for human consumption.

A dozen or so rather muddy pigs that had been occupying their time by snuffling around in the earth, came up and looked at us so expectantly and seemed so genuinely pleased to see us, that I almost felt like apologising to them in advance for all of the sheer rubbish that I was about to feed them.

"What are they called?" I asked, expecting that at least one would be called something appropriate, like 'Porky'.

"We call these *pigs*," was the rather brusque and humiliating response.

I felt like explaining myself but I could not bear risking the possibility of Mrs Greenwood making me appear even more stupid than she already had.

"Did you wanna give the food to the pigs?" she asked.

Geraldine happily replied, "Yes."

Mrs Greenwood then took the bucket from me and assisted Geraldine – who was only a little taller than the pigs were – as she lifted the bucket onto the top of the fence.

"All right then, love. There you go. Toss it all in," Mrs Greenwood instructed, intending (presumably) that the bucket should merely be tilted a little in order to expel its contents into the sty.

Unfortunately, the bucket was precariously balanced and as Geraldine tried to tilt it in order to get the 'food' out, the pigs became more excited.

Mrs Greenwood nevertheless urged her on, which made Geraldine panic and accidentally drop the bucket as well as the 'food' onto the wrong side of the fence, whereupon the animals immediately wasted no time in proceeding to tuck ravenously into their latest pile of edible rubbish.

Mrs Greenwood next introduced us to some new terms that we had not heard before – at least not from her – which were not particularly of endearment or farming related. She concluded with a very simple either-or question-and-answer session whereby we had to choose between *either* one of us girls going into the pen and retrieving the bucket that the pigs were all fighting over. *or* we were not going to have any lunch! After emptying the contents of the other bucket into the sty, Mrs Greenwood stood eagerly to attention, awaiting a decision from us.

I looked at my uncomfortable eight- and three-year-old companions, and then looked up at Mrs Greenwood and realised that all eyes were on me, which did not seem quite fair to say the least. My two younger associates were certainly unsuitable for a little trip inside the sty, while the adult who

71

was present was merely unwilling. However, I thought that I was not particularly up to such a task either, but I could see little alternative to my volunteering for it if I wanted to have lunch.

A minute or two after the bucket had been dropped inside the sty, things seemed to begin quietening down. Mrs Greenwood stood by the gate, ready to open it, and glared at me until I reluctantly approached her.

"Come on, come on. We 'aven't got all day," she said, impatient for the return of her beloved pail.

I plucked up the courage to enter the rather frenzied porcine mêlée and made my way towards the gate.

It had been a good life, I thought as I took that 'final' short walk towards the potential sty of doom – but then I thought again, and no, it had not. What a way to go, I lamented – 'snuffled' to death!

As I stood beside the gate, the other side of which lay the dropped bucket, Mrs Greenwood suddenly thrust it wide open before I was ready and almost pushed me straight to the other side of the enclosure. She then quickly closed the gate behind me, although she did kindly stand ready to open it again, just in case I was ever to return.

I virtually flew past the bucket, screaming all the way. I managed to pick it up and turn around without slipping over on the quite significant quantities of slush that made up much of the enclosure. I then ran back towards the entrance. Mrs Greenwood considerately opened the gate for me as I approached her. As I dashed past and outside the pen, she wasted no time firmly slamming it shut again behind me.

She then tossed into the pen the few remaining scraps that were still left in the bucket, and walked back to the farmhouse, demanding that we should all follow her. Doris saw me shiver a bit and we all realised immediately that we were certainly not at home any more – Mrs Greenwood was going to show little loving maternal instinct towards us. I felt that we girls really did only have each other to rely on for compassion in the future.

Detention in the field
As we neared the farmhouse, Mrs Greenwood's arm became outstretched and we were directed to return to our field, where we were to remain until she was to relent and allow us back out of it.

Doris, Geraldine and I withdrew there for the rest of the morning. We did not bother doing any more chasing of wildlife and, if anything, we began to feel a certain affinity with the other incarcerated animals that were on the farm.

"How long do you think we'll have to stay in here for?" asked a resigned Geraldine, resting her chin on a fence post and her hands over the same bar.

"Just until lunchtime… I hope," I replied, assuming that Mrs Greenwood would not harbour feelings of hostility towards us for longer than an hour or so.

Nevertheless, we all agreed to chance our luck by returning to the farmhouse for lunch and other necessities when all of the other farm workers would be going in, if we had not been released from our captivity by then.

Lunchtime…
We slunk into the farmhouse when we saw the farm-men entering it as well. We immediately saw places set around the food table for all of the workers and Mrs Greenwood but we saw nothing for three little girls who were guilty only of being incapable of holding a heavy bucket high up, on a fence.

Mrs Greenwood stared at us and all went quiet in the kitchen, so I took Doris' hand and Geraldine's, and led both of my apprehensive companions quickly towards the outside toilet. Afterwards, we sneaked back inside and upstairs to our bedroom.

When we later heard a lot of commotion outside, we

assumed that everyone had left, so we sneaked downstairs to the kitchen again but we were shocked to be suddenly confronted by Mrs Greenwood, who must have been waiting for us.

"Getting 'ungry now, are we girls?" she asked as we guiltily stood to attention by the entrance.

I nervously replied, "Yes."

The other girls responded likewise. Mrs Greenwood then put down three plates with a salad sandwich upon each.

"Well, you'd better eat those then," she said as she left the room and went briskly into the lounge.

We quietly sat down at the three laid places and began to eat our lunches. All of the time that we were there, the only sounds that we made were the munching of the vegetables or the occasional muffled 'Oh' murmurs as remnants of food tried escaping from between the two thick slices of bread that we were each awkwardly grasping.

When we were finishing our sandwiches, Mrs Greenwood re-entered the room and began talking about the animals.

"If you like the pigs, you can feed 'em every day," she said.

"They're quite aggressive," I exclaimed.

"Not if you feed 'em proper," she quickly replied. "You'll get used to 'em... in time." She hesitated, then added, "Don't go getting too attached to 'em, mind. They're not pets... and neither are the chickens. We'll give those a go later."

What Mrs Greenwood had just hinted at, I had always known – that all of the animals on the farm were destined to make the ultimate sacrifice for our country's dinner tables. Mrs Greenwood had unfortunately brought those negative thoughts to the fore and it took me some time to return them to the back of my mind.

I asked Mrs Greenwood where the post box was, so that we could send the postcards, which we had been given the previous day, back to our mother. I declined her offer to post them for me. I thought that Mrs Greenwood had been empowered enough as it was; I did not want her to be able to stop me communicating with my mother or to be able to dictate what I was to write. It would have made her too powerful, too domineering, and her presence, quite intolerable.

"All right then, Lilian. I'll show you later if you like," she said, with a certain curious intonation in her voice. In the meantime, she was going to take us to the chickens.

She was taking us to the chickens!

When we had all finished our food and drink, we followed Mrs Greenwood to the chicken coop. Inside the modest shed-like structure, standing around and fidgeting on a couple of shelves that were approximately five and six feet high, there were about ten black-feathered chickens and four colourful cockerels. The latter had black lower halves, a golden-brown upper plumage and bright pink heads. The oldest cockerels, we were told, were the ones with the longest protrusions – known as 'spurs' – at the backs of their legs.

About three feet from the ground, there was the main platform, which was covered in straw. The chickens laid their eggs there, often hiding them underneath the straw. Although the poultry could manage a little leap up a foot or so when they gave their wings a bit of a zealous flap, a wooden slope had been placed against the platform in order to assist them in their ascent up to it.

Eggs are laid from early in February until the autumn. Healthy chickens – a good indicator of which is a fine plumage – tend to lay once a day. Thus, the ten chickens, which looked healthy enough, gave Mrs Greenwood a daily yield of about eight to ten eggs.

There was a problem, though, with other birds entering the coop and thieving the eggs, so white clay 'eggs' were placed on the platform. If any intruding birds ever thieved them, then the Greenwood's would only have lost a virtually worthless item and not something as valuable as a real egg! Another advantage of using the clay eggs was that they encouraged the chickens to do their laying where their eggs could be most easily collected every day, which was on the platform. That was because the chickens tended to copy each other, so they would lay next to where other chickens appeared to have already laid.

At the side of the coop, there was a container with corn seeds and a scoop in it. The corn – which consisted of wheat, maize and barley – was all destined for the poultry. Mrs Greenwood filled the scoop with the seeds and then sprinkled them over the ground outside. That day, the poultry initially declined their food... *"Oh, no thank you. Not today, Mrs G. Couldn't possibly. Full up, you know. Cluck!"*

They seemed nervous and unwilling to leave the safety of their coop, possibly because of the unusual presence of us girls. However, a wave of Mrs Greenwood's arm in their direction soon encouraged them to vacate their sanctuary and go outside for the meal.

We stood and watched for about ten minutes as the birds heartily clucked and pecked at their seeds. Mrs Greenwood urged us girls to do likewise (to feed the poultry, that is, not join in with them), which we successfully did.

About twenty yards away, at the end of the yard, Mr Greenwood was standing with Bobby the dog. Mr Greenwood urged Bobby in our direction and then began giving various whistles and calls to it. Bobby responded to the commands by eagerly circling the erstwhile contented birds and driving the poor things back into the coop – after we had only just spent ages trying to get them to leave it!

"'E may be a sheepdog... but 'e can round up my chickens just as good," Mr Greenwood proudly boasted as he came up to us.

"Well done, girls. Thank you. Now, who wants to do that in future?" Mrs Greenwood asked.

We looked at Bobby and then pursed our lips, trying to make the same kind of noises that Mr Greenwood had just made.

"Not the whistling thing! I meant the feeding of the chickens," groaned Mrs Greenwood, frustrated at our misunderstanding.

"Oh!" the girls and I replied, feeling slightly foolish.

Doris and Geraldine immediately spoke up, saying that they wanted to do it.

"You're too late, Lilian. The other girls have beaten you to it," Mrs Greenwood said, with a sense of satisfaction.

I was not particularly upset that Doris and Geraldine would be feeding the chickens – at least not until Mrs Greenwood said that that now meant that I would be feeding the pigs from now on! I suddenly felt that I had just been the helpless victim of some clever trickery. What cunning, I thought. Mrs Greenwood had given the first girls to volunteer, the better job to do; meanwhile, the child who hesitated had ended up with the worst!

How much more work on the farm, I wondered, was to be assigned to us girls using such a clever form of skulduggery as asking us who wanted to do it. I was determined not to allow myself to be outwitted by the shrewd Mrs Greenwood in future... although I feared that I probably would be.

Letting mother know where we were

That evening, we sat in our room and wrote little messages on our postcards. Our teacher had previously warned us only to write cheerful things, so as not to upset our mother (or parents, in the case of Geraldine). It was an attitude with which I was still somewhat able to concur. Consequently, Doris and I wrote things like 'We are having lots of fun with the animals' and 'We've been happily playing in the fields with our new friend Geraldine.'

Mrs Greenwood entered the room as we were writing and asked us if we were 'All going to start crying again tonight?' adding that we had kept her awake for much of the previous night with some of our 'noises'. We promised that she would not hear any further sounds from us at night.

The next day, we sent our postcards back home to our families, thereby letting them know where their daughters had been taken and assuring them that we were all still well, although we were missing them very much.

Learning more about the farm

After lunch, Mr Greenwood spent a couple of hours giving all of us children a guided tour of the farm. We saw a hand-operated water pump and, near that, a plough, which was pulled along by the farm's two large and powerful horses. The animals were in good health and – unlike the tractor, which often broke down – they needed neither petrol nor spare parts to work – only food!

Next to the plough was a similar device, which had metal discs instead of scoops. It was used to break up the newly ploughed earth. Nearby, there was a potato-planting contraption, which planted the crop into the furrow that had just been created.

In a large shed farther along the yard, we were shown a small box with a thin bar attached, which was used for sowing seed such as wheat. When the bar was pulled to the right – in a similar fashion to that of a bow on a violin, from whence the whole device acquired its name of 'seed fiddle' – a hole at the bottom of the mechanism opened, which would allow a seed to fall to the ground. The size of the hole could be adjusted to accommodate seeds of various sizes. Although it used only simple weights, levers and other things, it proved to be quite an ingenious little semi-automated sowing device.

Mr Greenwood next showed us where he made cider. The

milling device first ripped the pieces of apples into a kind of mush and then straw was added to it before it was put into a second device, known as the 'press'.

"*Straw?*" we exclaimed, the moment that it was mentioned. We wondered why anyone would want to make a drink with straw in it... "*Fine drink of cider you've done here, Mr Greenwood... and some lovely straw you've put in it as well. Cheers!*"

And what if Mr Greenwood was about to show us any other kinds of drink that he was used to making on the farm – one, for instance, that came 'with a good head on it'. That was one lecture in brewing that I definitely would not wish to attend!

Eventually, Mr Greenwood was able to explain to his little rowdy audience that the pulped apples (more accurately referred to as 'pomace') only had the straw added as a temporary measure, which was while a press was squeezing the juice out of them. Without the straw to hold the pomace together, he said, the pieces of apple would just fall out of the machine.

A filter sat on top of a churn and it was through that filter that the pomace juice was poured. Virtually all of the debris – such as loose apple lumps or bits of straw – was caught by it, thereby allowing only 'pure' juice to enter the vessel. Any cider drunk straight from the press, Mr Greenwood assured us, was highly potent and would often result in 'soiled pants in the morning'! The apple juice would finally be transferred to two oak barrels. After fermenting for a few months, it would turn into cider! The remaining pomace could be fed to the pigs or chickens. Half of a beetroot was usually put into the cider but that was only in order to improve the appearance of it – Mr Greenwood said that it does not affect the taste.

The resultant coloured cider was actually quite weak in terms of its alcohol content, which was probably beneficial when it came to supplying it to the farm labourers. It was meant, after all, to keep them going and be a treat for them while they carried out their hard work. It was not supposed to be too inebriating. Had it been so, the unfortunate possibility would arise that the workers would eventually collapse in the fields or wander around in a kind of daze – an interminable merry stupor. It would be a change in his workforce's behaviour that, Mr Greenwood assured us, he would notice... *"Way, hey... Let's all gather the harvest in, lads... Wee! Hiccup!"*

A glass of the cider was often also given as a 'perk' to people who arrived at the farm to deliver things.

We next ventured to the farm's slurry pit, which was about ten feet high and fifty yards in diameter, and was used for storing various waste matter that was to be spread on the fields.

The last place that we were shown that day was a large shed that contained a red mechanical corn crusher. It supplied crushed barley that was then mixed with water in order to make a kind of 'porridge', which was given to the cows and pigs in winter.

Mr Greenwood then spoke about the cows' diet, which

included hay (dried grass) and silage. Silage is grass that has been cut and left to wilt in the sun, and is then collected and 'clamped' (which means that it is stored in a pit, known as a clamp). The sugars and other chemicals that it naturally contains eventually pickle it.

Mr Greenwood also mentioned wheat straw and barley straw, which he used for animal bedding. He gave us quite an education that afternoon about many different farming matters, and left us all appreciating a lot more of the work that he and the others on the farm had to do every day, seven days a week... fifty-two weeks of the year.

Messages from home

A few days after we had sent our postcards to our homes, Geraldine, Doris and I all got responses from our families. Coincidentally, the letter from Geraldine's parents arrived at the same time as my mother's.

Geraldine opened her letter moments before Doris and I opened ours, and I immediately saw her break down in tears. I went over to her and put my hand on her shoulder.

When I began to read the letter from my mother, I now started to cry; and when I looked at Doris, I saw that she had begun bawling as well. We were all clearly not having the happiest of times. I left Geraldine and went over to comfort Doris instead.

The letters that were causing such emotions were, nevertheless, welcome communications. They confirmed, as if we needed such assurances, that we had not been forgotten. Moreover, they were timely – if hurtful – reminders of the love that we all now found so wanting.

5

An education

Back to "school"

WITHIN DAYS OF our arrival at the farm, an official visited in order to make arrangements for us children to start attending the local school. A week later, Mrs Greenwood accompanied us on our first journey there. Doris was too young to start school yet, so she remained on the farm.

Following the same route that we had taken only a few days earlier, we passed familiar animals that were still doing nothing except grazing nonchalantly in their fields. From high in the trees, the mild morning air carried sweet, bright birdsong. Meanwhile, wild flowering plants – silhouetted against the clear, blue sky – towered high above us and swayed leisurely on the gentle, melodic breeze. Lower down, by our passing feet, regiments of small, pretty, living colours of the rainbow – attended to by the occasional industrious bee – lay with a graceful presence throughout our long and picturesque trail.

It was almost as if all of nature knew that we were on our way to start at a new school and she was endeavouring to begin the day for us as pleasantly as possible. Her splendid sweeping efforts gently touched the senses; they were spiritually uplifting and gratefully received.

Mrs Greenwood returned to the farm when we reached the school. I recognised one of the teachers there as being from my old school but others, we were later to find out, were temporary replacements for those who were unable, or perhaps unwilling, to be evacuated to the area. Geraldine and I went over to a couple of my old school friends, Emily and Sarah, to have a chat and to find out how they had been settling in so far. It turned out that their experiences of the evacuation so far – at least in the emotional sense – were not very different from mine.

When the school bell rang, all of the local schoolchildren and all of those who had been evacuated to the area before us, lined up in the playground and then went, as directed, into the school. For the rest of us – all from many different schools – the small building was quite inadequate.

Eventually, as the fine summer weather was still holding, it was decided that our education was going to start there and then – in the playground! Some blackboards, easels, chalks and dusters were produced from inside the building, as were chairs for the teachers. Meanwhile we children had to make do with sitting on the cool, hard concrete. Our new open 'classroom' was one of several created there that morning, all in close proximity to each other.

Nature trail...

The following week, all of the school's evacuees went on a nature trail, to learn about various plants and animals. I tended to stay with Emily and Sarah – and Geraldine, who was from a class of younger children but who took the opportunity to spend much of the day with me for a change.

At a peaceful, gentle, little river, Miss Hillary, my teacher, began pointing at some large birds paddling along on the water.

"Those birds there..." she said, pointing at them, "... they're called Canada geese and those ducks over there..." she said, pointing now at them, "... they're called mallards."

We all stood quietly, looking down at the Canada geese and the mallards and then up again at Miss Hillary, expecting her to come out with some more of her learned words of wisdom, although she uncharacteristically fell silent for a few moments. I thought that her nature lesson was about to end there, when a pair of large, graceful swans made a sudden, unexpected appearance from farther along the river.

"Look at those..." she said, joyously, "... those lovely, big, white birds coming our way. Can you all see them?"

"Yes," we said, not surprisingly.

One swan stopped for a moment, to stretch and audibly flap its wings.

"Well, they're swans and I think that they're called, mute swans."

"Mute," many of us repeated back.

"What does mute mean?" one boy asked.

"It means they don't talk, doesn't it, Miss?" another boy interjected, displaying a prior knowledge of the definition of silence.

"That's right," acknowledged Miss Hillary.

"So which birds *do* talk?" asked another inquisitive child.

"Well, the ducks go 'quack' and that's a kind of talking, isn't it children?" she said, which we all took as our cue to begin quacking for the next thirty seconds or so.

"All right then children, that's enough quacking," Miss Hillary declared, holding her hands up to her ears as the sounds of the endless quacks slowly faded away. "Did you know, children, that swans stay together for life?"

"No," we all said, being not very well acquainted with avian domestic arrangements.

"If one dies, the other will probably just pine away. It will just stop eating and die of a broken heart," she added poignantly.

"Ahhh..." we all said sadly, empathising with the doomed swan pair – one fated to die first, the other expected to fade away soon after, lonely and heartbroken, following a prolonged period of physical and emotional deterioration. A pleasant stroll through the countryside had become decidedly grimmer of late, I thought.

"Shall we stay for a while and have our lunch here? It seems a pleasant enough place," Miss Hillary asked rhetorically as she lowered herself onto the grassy bank, to rest for a while from the rambles and nature studies.

While we were eating our packed lunches and drinking our bottles of lemonade or water, we watched the amusing wildlife – the ducks, in particular. They regularly plunged, head first, to feed vertically on the river bottom, but they had to paddle frantically with their feet in order to stay upside down. They became far more active near us when someone threw them a piece of bread.

"Don't do that!" was Miss Hillary's immediate rebuke. She reliably informed everyone that the birds would have loved to have eaten all of our bread but that there was a war on and we should not waste food on animals that already had all that they needed to eat, in and around their own river.

Some of the boys went too close to the river. They were soon warned to stay away from it in case they fell in. Elsewhere, other children made small toy boats out of twigs, which were tied together with long grass and then had large leaves added for sails. They were then carefully lowered onto the water using long, hooked twigs (the boats were, not the children) but they only travelled a few feet before disintegrating.

Sarah suddenly exclaimed, "Look at those!" as she saw about half a dozen fluffy cute little ducklings nearby, chasing after their parents.

The parent ducks were waddling slowly along the riverbank but their many ducklings were encumbered with only little legs and they were struggling to keep up. The parents then stopped and carefully, if not very gracefully, plopped themselves into the river.

Within a few seconds, the ducklings came alongside

their parents. They hesitated. Then, one after the other, they plopped, rolled or bounced their way down the short, sloping bank and entered the river as well. When only one of the ducklings had still not entered the water, the parent ducks and their brood started to move off. The last duckling, not wishing to be left behind, found courage: it leapt out, splashed into the water and joined his (or her) brothers and sisters again. The family, together once more, continued their journey just as nature had intended – bobbing along on the water and quacking away happily.

After lunch, we were all taken to a large heath. There, Miss Hillary assured us that any snakes spotted would not be venomous although toadstools, which look virtually identical to mushrooms, would make us very ill if we touched or ate them. Were we all going to leave the place alive, many of us began to wonder.

We were given a quick lecture on beautiful butterflies, and invited to use Miss Hillary's pocket reference book to identify the different species that we could see fluttering about, whose appearance we immediately forgot as our mass of children instantly exploded in all directions in search of them.

As Miss Hillary later began to lead us all slowly out of the heath, she spoke of the seasons and how they affected nature, and highlighted the scattering of the purple plants that lightly covered the heath. They were just one part of nature's wonderful plan, she said, to make the countryside beautiful, colourful and attractive for all children – to encourage us to come and explore it, and delight in its splendour.

At the edge of the heath, it became very wooded and dark because of the thick overhanging branches of the tall trees that were growing there. We were told not to enter the 'grove' (as Miss Hillary called it), as she did not want any of us hurting ourselves or becoming lost in it. We could only stand at the opening for a few minutes and stare despondently. (We were not instructed to stare despondently – we just did.)

Before returning to school, we were offered one final treat – a visit to the village pond. From a distance, we saw ducks bobbing about on the water and frogs sitting contentedly on floating lily pads. However, when we arrived they inextricably started jumping into the water, so that within a matter of only a few seconds they had all gone. Moments later, the two enormous eyes (relatively speaking) of each frog slowly started to surface and peer at us. I presumed they were waiting for us to leave their environment, when they would feel safe to return fully to the surface.

"Look Lily, there's another one!" Geraldine would say as each one popped up from below.

Occasionally, the odd little bird landed on one of the pads and ate any insects that it found on it. Suddenly, one of the boys threw a stone into the pond, which unfortunately made all of the frogs go back below the surface again.

"Ohhh..." we all said – at least those of us who liked watching nature.

For his unkind act towards the pond wildlife, Miss Hillary warned the boy that he might not be allowed out on any more nature trips in future. He seemed to behave himself more after that.

A couple of frogs by the edge of the pond, which were almost hidden by overhanging growth, seemed relatively unmoved by our arrival and, unlike their fellow amphibians, they seemed disinclined to enter the water – even after the boy's projectile had landed near them. Another unusual aspect of their behaviour was that they appeared to be clinging onto each other or, to be more precise, one was clinging on tightly to the other.

"They're frightened," Miss Hillary said. "That's why they're doing that. You're frightening them and you should leave them both alone."

That, of course, only made us all even more curious and inclined to go up to them, to see what 'frightened' frogs looked like. After we had all had a quick peek at the two frightened frogs, we left them alone to recover from the experience (the frogs were to recover, that is, not us) and began making our way back to school.

Change of school venue
After a couple of weeks of making do with the playground for a classroom, my fellow evacuees and I were given the use of the local village hall for our lessons. By the doorway, there was a line of buckets. Some contained sand, while the others had water. There was also a little contraption called a stirrup-pump. All of these items, we were very strictly told, were not to be interfered with at all by us. They always had to be available for fighting fires.

We were immediately put to work, sticking black tape in long, diagonal, criss-cross patterns over all of the windows, to prevent the glass fragmenting and flying everywhere if a German bomb was to fall and explode nearby during an air raid.

Although there had been no war to speak of until then – at least as far as I was aware – we were still always required to carry our gas masks. We were told that in a real gas attack, we would only have a matter of a few seconds in which to put our masks on and that if we took too long, the gas could severely injure or even kill us!

In order to test our preparedness, once a week (to begin with) we all had to practice our gas-mask drill, when Miss Hillary – at any time of the day and without warning – would give the alarm in a high-pitched voice: "Gas! Gas! Gas!"

After a month or so, a rudimentary air-raid shelter was built at the back of the hall, which gave us somewhere safe to go to when any future air-raid drills were organised.

The art of war

Notable attempts were made to continue giving us all a proper education despite quite adverse circumstances. However, after a while we began receiving replacement teachers who covered for when Miss Hillary was not available, which was perhaps two or three times a week.

The teachers sometimes spent their time telling us about the great exploits, which were apparently taking place, of the allied armed forces. Afterwards, we were invited to do paintings or drawings of the poignant events mentioned. Generally, only the boys found that kind of subject matter interesting.

They produced stark landscapes filled with the abhorrent smoky grey and blood-red colours of the darkest inhumanities of war; and seascapes of dramatic battles, where foundering wrecks of ignominious Nazi U-boats were beginning their final descents to the deep while victorious Royal Navy warships circled triumphantly around their dying prey. Sweeping across a pellucid sky, noble RAF fighters were assuredly destroying the advancing storms of winged cohorts of the black cross and swastika.

I liked art and my love of it grew as time went on, but I could far more comfortably express my artistic tendencies when we were allowed to do pictures of the flora and fauna that we had so often come across. Then, for a change, pleasant images were depicted – of the beauty and variety of the nature that surrounded us. On those afternoons, my palette lit up with bright, innocent colours; my 'canvas' (a sheet of paper, actually) shone with an explosion of multicoloured blooms. My imagination was set free on a sea of placid verdancy. With spreads of yellows, high puffs of whites, brown boughs and patches of pink faces, and gay mixtures of all of the other colours that I had been given, a majestic nature grew: a world that I wanted to see and be a part of – of harmless hues and infinite tranquillity – and I escaped into it.

6

Country life matters

For king and country!
GERALDINE AND I had to carry out a few farm duties after school, one of which was to pick up any eggs that we found lying around the coop. Doris often helped us. To make the work seem less of a chore, we sometimes competed to see who could collect the most but we had to handle them very carefully, especially if they were being retrieved from underneath the chickens, for woe betide the person who dropped any of Mrs Greenwood's precious eggs!

Occasionally – when a hen was suspiciously clucking and fidgeting about a lot, or looking so chubby that it must surely, we thought, have been about to lay – we decided to sit and wait a while for the apparently overdue egg to pop out. Before long, we would be eagerly urging the retentive hen to deliver her little important package, and comparing her modest endeavours to those of the other chickens that we assumed had already served the wider national cause of helping to feed a country short of food.

"Come on. Do it for king and country," I might have urged occasionally, hoping that I would inflame an unresponsive bird's sense of patriotism and duty, and thereby encourage her to complete the simple production of just one more egg.

Once, Doris was overcome by the excitement of the occasion. Wishing to do her bit for the war effort, she picked up such a hen and began giving it a bit of a shake as though that was all that was needed for one more egg to plop out.

Impassioned, Geraldine urged, "Come on 'henny'. Do it for King George."

To the chorus of heartfelt exhortations, I contributed, "Go on, hen. The king wants your egg," but still our chicken maintained its reluctance to lay anything.

Our vocal encouragements alone appeared inadequate; the bird seemed unmoved by our earnest supplications. Geraldine then suggested that Doris should give it a bit of a squeeze – to 'help nature along', as she put it.

"No!" I said, stopping her quickly. I did not think that 'henny' was too happy with all of the personal egg-laying encouragements that she was already receiving. I dreaded to think what would have happened if my sister had started squeezing her.

"I don't think the hen's going to lay an egg," I added profoundly, ending the sorry proceedings at that point. Geraldine and Doris were clearly disappointed.

"Traitor!" Doris called the hen, as she lowered it back to the floor.

"We're gonna tell George the Sixth about you!" added Geraldine, pointing and looking sternly at the apathetic chicken as we began to make our way out of the chicken coop and back to the farmhouse with all of the eggs that we had managed to collect.

Chickens don't just give us eggs...
We ate a meat-based meal at least once a week, the origins of which were the home-grown livestock or some of the animals that were caught trespassing on our farm.

Usually, the rabbits that were brought into the farmhouse had died some hours earlier but the chickens were killed just beforehand. The boys from our farm would chase after and catch one or two, and then the burly farmer broke their necks (the chickens' necks, that is, not the boys'). It was quite disturbing, for some time afterwards, to watch the unfortunate birds continue to flap their wings about through what was termed 'a reflex action', and, although 'dead', behave as though they were still alive.

The sounds of the pigs being killed were distressing enough but the witnessing of it proved more than this eleven-year-old girl wished to bear. Afterwards, their carcasses were hung on a hook on the chimney-breast, to turn them into smoked bacon.

I had to help Mrs Greenwood with the cooking, and usually emerged from such times in the kitchen with several unwelcome spurts of blood over my dress. When the meal was nearly cooked, Geraldine or I carefully laid out the plates or bowls on the table. The largest items of crockery were placed where the adults would be sitting and the smallest were laid where the children would sit.

If any people from the farm were still outside when the food was ready, Mrs Greenwood would take a pan and a big spoon out to the doorstep. She would then bash them together (the pan and the spoon, that is, not the people outside who had not come in yet) while screaming in a high-pitched voice, "Meals out!"

More farm duties

The boys who were evacuated to the farm with us tended to do the hard, physical outdoor work such as clearing out the animal sheds, tidying up the farmyard or working in the fields. We girls, on the other hand, were generally given things inside the farmhouse to do, such as the laundry, the washing up and general tidying. We also made small jam sandwiches or buns for the other farm workers, and carried the food to wherever they were on the farm. If they were nearby, we would sometimes take a drink to them as well.

They usually took some large, brown and grey jars of cider out with them if they were going a long way. Drinking from one was difficult: two or three fingers from one hand, which was bent back, held the handle while the weight of the vessel was taken by the forearm and elbow. The cider poured out (with luck, into one's mouth!) when the elbow was raised.

We sometimes made loaves of bread and, if we were lucky – when provisions allowed – we were able to make lovely cakes with fillings of cream and toppings of icing. Sometimes, the meals had unusual names. One that we did consisted of potatoes and cabbages, and occasionally other bits of spare food that we had. All were mashed together and fried, and the result – 'bubble and squeak' – did not taste at all bad.

Once, when I had been moaning to Mrs Greenwood more than usual about all of work that I was doing, she punished me by making me go outside and collect nettles, to make into nettle soup. Unfortunately, although I was wearing gloves, I still managed to get stung several times and that only made me complain even more. I did eventually stop my protests, though, when I was told that practice makes perfect and I was asked if I wanted to go outside again and try picking some more. For all of my modest efforts, the final concoction that we produced, although tolerable, was far from the most wonderful thing that I have ever tasted.

Christmas... of a sort

The snows of winter came. Farm animals, unable to find grass to eat, were moved into warm barns. Meanwhile, the transformed landscape of delightful soft whiteness now became a huge playground for us children.

Christmas Day itself meant eating especially well for a change, although things had not been particularly bad before. Several local people, including the families of the other farm workers, turned up for an arranged feast. It was held in the kitchen and the lounge; in the latter, a welcome roaring fire was maintained to keep out the cold of a sharp winter's day.

Despite ample quantities of farm-made cider being

available for the adults, still more alcohol was liberally supplied by those visiting us. Before long, one of the workers felt inspired to delight the inebriated with his hearty rendition of pieces of 'music' that he 'played' on an old violin. Apparently, the intoxicated revellers automatically recognised every misplayed note of the violin, for they sang along with almost uncanny synchronised imperfection. Those who remained sober (a minority group, which now just consisted of us children) were not party to the invaluable effects of the alcohol.

A kind of barn dance ensued, where everyone was invited to 'doh-si-doh' but alcohol or youthful inexperience meant that there was little proper co-ordination. It was pleasant enough, though.

Doris, Geraldine and I eventually retired to our room, where we were allowed to play with Mr Greenwood's cards by lamplight until relatively late. We then lay in bed for another hour or so, listening involuntarily to the noises that were still emanating from the party downstairs and feeling as though we were now being sorely punished for some recent terrible misdemeanour.

'Screech, screech, sing, sing,' came up to bedevil our every audio-sensory nerve. Then it came again: 'Screech, screech, sing, sing, screech, screech.' We wondered if it would *ever* stop.

The boys down the hall, who had gone to their room just after us, now bravely spoke out a couple of times to the revellers below with calls of, "Shut up," and, "Stop playing that f*****g violin."

They were probably wise, though, in making their fully justified protestations just inaudible to the adults – especially the Greenwoods, who would almost certainly have taken offence at such impudence from one of their evacuees.

The girls and I began to wonder if the hosts had specially invited an alternative, out-of-tune violin troupe specialising in screeching impressions of an ageing, asthmatic cat being swung around by another ageing, asthmatic cat, all to the heartily expressed vocal joy of a couple of impersonators of deaf, hyperactive baritone piglets.

When such a surreal performance was to the singular delight of twenty or so drunk guests, who all seemed captivated by the 'splendour' of the imagined performing menagerie, I had to conclude that they really were such a troupe... or perhaps it only appeared that way to three very tired girls who were just trying to get to sleep after a very long Christmas Day.

I eventually fell asleep to the sounds of drunks intermittently leaving the farmhouse and slamming the squeaky door behind them after first thanking their hosts for a 'grand' or 'splendid' evening.

A time to decide

With the passing months, more and more of my fellow evacuees were returning home. British cities – being left alone by the Germans – were apparently not dangerous places after all; the war was 'phoney'. As I became ever more uneasy about all of the killings of the animals on the farm, and as London looked increasingly attractive, I wrote to my mother, informing her that I was seriously considering going back there. Although she repeated her hopeful requests that I could remain on the farm, to look after Doris, she eventually sent me the funds that I needed for the rail journey home. Fortunately, the Greenwoods did not open my mail, so I was able to keep my plans secret for as long as I needed.

I told Doris about my desire to leave but, unfortunately, as soon as I said how much our mother wanted us to remain on the farm while the war was still going on, she did not display the same determination to leave that I had. It seemed more likely that her young years had not given her the will to leave, rather than she had such a desire to stay; nevertheless, her decision put me in quite a personal dilemma. That afternoon – to clear my head – I went for a walk around the fields on my own.

It seemed to me that if my constitution would not allow me to stay, then I would just have to go and, anyway, I knew that Doris was with the Greenwoods, so I would at least be leaving her in relatively safe hands. They had not seemed too bad a family until now, so if she did stay, then it could not exactly be said that I was abandoning my sister.

I went to visit the sheep in their cosy barn.

"Sheep!" I called but they tended to just move away. I leant over the cold metal barrier and stroked their woollen coats for a moment.

"Goodbye, sheep," I said but they just ignored me and carried on moving out of reach.

Then I got a 'bah' out of one of them, so I decided to remain near that more talkative one for a while. The sheep – all being sheep – had long heads and almost looked as depressed as I felt; theirs seemed another place of weighty contemplation.

I gave the vocal young lamb a 'bah' back from me – a first sign of a kindred spirit, perhaps.

Then Mrs Greenwood found me and called out for me to go back indoors. I patted the sheep that was closest to me – the only one that I could actually reach – on the top of its long, thoughtful head, and slowly walked away. The early winter sunset was changing the colours of the land. Whites were turning to grey; dark greys to black; and a light, cloudy sky was hanging over everything. It was time to go home.

The next day, when I told my school friends about my plan to go home that weekend, they advised me to go without saying anything to the teachers in case attempts would be made to try to stop me leaving. My friends said that they would explain my absence to them after I had gone home.

That afternoon, back on the farm, I announced to Mrs

Greenwood my intention of returning home that weekend. When I explained my loathing of the killing of the animals, and my desire to get back to my natural environment, there was little else to be said.

The last day
On that last Saturday, Mrs Greenwood woke me up unusually early to ensure – as she put it – that I would not miss the train

home. She said that as petrol was now for essential matters only and, on her farm, I was not 'essential' (and I probably did not particularly 'matter' all that much either!), I was not going to be given a lift to the railway station. However, one of the farm workers – Henry – would accompany me, to prevent me 'getting lost or into trouble', and he might also carry some of my things for me if I was to ask him nicely.

After breakfast, Doris asked me if we could feed the animals together. Mrs Greenwood looked away as I said, "Yes, let's," so, after we had finished our bowls of porridge, we went to leave the farmhouse.

Suddenly, Mrs Greenwood looked at me and said, "Oh, so you still wanna *feed* the animals, then?"

I just said yes and went outside with Doris.

Geraldine cried out, "Wait for me", which we did as she hurriedly finished her breakfast. She then shoved the bowl away, pushed her chair back and dashed outside to join us.

"Bye, bye, pigs," I said as – for one last time – I gave my pigs more of the same old stuff, and thought, as I did so, how big some of them were getting.

Having long since mastered my fear of the chickens pecking my legs, I caught one in the coop and carefully held it firmly through the arch of my elbow. I stroked it for a minute before carefully lowering it back onto the floor. It scampered away very quickly, possibly very relieved.

"Bye, bye, chickens," I bade as I left her and her companions.

In the stables, where Daniel had just finished scraping grit from the horses' hooves, I took a brush from the wall and began proudly grooming the great beasts of burden with it. I always made sure that I stayed well clear of their hind legs, lest they should hit me as I worked away but the horses never did hurt me. They were friendly, and both they and I always seemed to enjoy the grooming experience.

"Bye, bye, sheep," I said, after running over to their pen.

I managed to pat a couple goodbye, but they all just moved away, almost as though they were becoming fed up with me, every few days, going up to them and patting them on their heads!

Afterwards, Doris, Geraldine and I all went back into the farmhouse to finish packing my things for the journey home. As they were doing so, Doris and then Geraldine started crying and then that made me start to cry as well.

"I've got to go. I don't like it here anymore..." I said.

To Doris, I added, "... and if you feel the same way, get Mum to give you the money and come back as well." As I said it, though, I felt uncomfortable with Doris' expression – she was standing and looking back at me with an air of hopelessness. She then went to collect my old rag doll.

When she came back, to hand it to me, I was about to take it from her but I hesitated and, instead, I bade her, "*You* take it. You can look after her now... for the time being. You can be her Auntie Doris..."

I looked over at Geraldine and said, "... and you can be her Auntie Geraldine." That made them both smile.

"I'll give her back to you when I come home," declared Doris, faithfully.

"Look after her. I don't want her telling me that you've been mistreating her... telling her off for not eating all of her porridge," I added playfully.

Doris smiled and held the doll close. She looked at it, then climbed up to her bunk and laid it next to her doll.

"Look, Bessy – Elizabeth's not going after all!" she said, to which Bessy, the doll, sat up and replied, in a voice remarkably similar to Doris', 'Ooh, that's good. We can carry on playing together now then.'

Geraldine then climbed up her bunk, retrieved her golliwog, dog and cat dolls, came down and then climbed up Doris' bunk. Then, in voices that were very similar to Geraldine's as well as Doris', all of the dolls celebrated

Elizabeth's return to the 'family' – the distinguished house of fine cloth and rags.

"Hello, Elizabeth!" they all said, circling around her and bouncing up and down with joy. When Doris turned and smiled at me, while barely containing the excitement of the celebrations taking place on her bed, I was almost moved to climb up to Doris' bunk and start joining in with the celebrations as well. I hesitated.

I wanted all to be as it was, only a few months earlier. I wanted Doris to go home with me. We could have dumped the unnecessary luggage, used my fare money to get half way to London and just walked the rest of the way home, however far it would be. I felt sure that we could have managed it. I worried for poor Doris.

As we were packing, I left the girls anything of mine that they needed, saying that it made my suitcase lighter. However, as my large case was now only half-filled, it seemed sensible to leave it for Doris' later use and take her small one instead. I now proceeded to transfer everything of mine into it.

"Lilian, you're being really stupid," Doris uttered as she spent the next ten minutes helping me to unpack and then re-pack everything. The final item – as usual – was the gas mask, which we left sitting on top of everything in its now rather tired cardboard box.

"I suppose I'd better say goodbye to everyone," I said and, with that, we all filed downstairs and outside to where the farm workers sat 'doin' the cows', as Mrs Greenwood used to say.

I bade farewell to Mr Greenwood and Daniel, and to the other men in the barn who were milking the cows. I said goodbyes as well to the boys, who were busily sweeping up some hay in a barn.

"You still here?" asked Martin.

"Yes," I replied, rather pointlessly.

"Mrs Greenwood said you don't like 'em killing their animals," Bernard quipped.

"No, that's right," I said.

"Oh," said Alexander, who continued to sweep with a broom that was taller than he was.

"When are you going, then?" asked Martin.

"Right now!" interjected Doris.

"Does your mum know you're going back?" asked Alexander.

"Yes. She sent me the money for the train fare."

"You ever comin' back?"

"No, Roger," I replied.

"Well, see you around then," said Bernard, cordially, knowing that he almost certainly would *not* be seeing me around in the future.

"Bye then, Lilian," said Roger.

"Bye, Lilian," said Alexander.

"She's leaving us to do all the work now, lads. I don't know… Goodbye, Lily," said Martin, quickly resuming his labour of love, in and around the barn.

"Bye," I said once more to the boys as I turned smartly and walked away.

Mrs Greenwood suddenly appeared from the farmhouse, and drove proceedings on with her instruction, "All right then, Lilian. Go and get your stuff."

Back in my room, I looked through the window once more, at the view of the farm I was sure I would never see again. Doris and Geraldine stood beside me but none of us spoke. When I finished reminiscing, I collected my bag and gas mask, checked that I had everything and then went downstairs and outside again, closely followed by the girls.

"Bye, bye, Bobby," I said, when he appeared. I patted him on his head, and his tail wagged a bit. Then he nonchalantly wandered off once more into the farmyard.

"You'd better 'ave something before you go," Mrs

Greenwood said. She invited me back into the house for a cup of tea, and gave me a sandwich for the journey home.

"You know you can't come back if you leave. We'll be taking someone else in," she warned.

"I know," I said, having previously been told that by Mr Greenwood.

"Can we go with her?" Geraldine asked.

For a moment, my spirit was raised. I thought that Doris might actually be coming home with me. Then I realised that she and Geraldine only contemplated accompanying me as far as the railway station.

"Better see what 'enry thinks," said Mrs Greenwood, leading us back to the milking shed. "'Enry! When you're done, can you take Lilian, then?"

"OK," said Henry, who was now engrossed in milking another cow.

"And what about the other girls?" asked Mrs Greenwood. "They wanna go as well."

Henry appeared ready to disappoint my companions but then he saw their faces and had a change of heart. He agreed they could accompany me.

"Hooray!" cried Doris and Geraldine, jumping up and down a little in their moment of bridled joy.

"Mind, 'enry, if they start slowing you down, they'll 'ave to come straight back," warned Mrs Greenwood. She then left us girls by the milking shed and returned to the farmhouse.

After about ten minutes, Henry finished his milking. He got up, stretched his cramped legs a little and then came towards me.

"You all ready now then, Lilian?" he asked a little apprehensively, worried perhaps in case I was not.

"Ready," I said.

"Right, let's be off then," he swiftly declared.

Remembering what Mrs Greenwood had said earlier

about asking Henry nicely to carry my bag for me, I held it out towards him and then said, "Erm..."

"What is it, Lilian? Did you want me to carry it for you?" he asked perceptively.

"Yes, please."

With that, he kindly took my bag from me.

"Thank you," I said, courteously. As the girls and I began following him, I turned and bellowed, "Bye!" back to those people who were still around to see and hear me.

Mrs Greenwood, now standing next to her husband, raised her hand in acknowledgement. Mr Greenwood – who was still milking the cows – gave a friendly nod, as did one of the other men in the shed. Then I turned around again and continued on my way, leaving the farm and all of its affairs behind me. My loyal, supportive companions – Geraldine and Doris – remained by my side. I was glad to have their company – especially Doris' – even if it was only for just another hour or two.

As we made our way briskly along numerous country lanes, Doris, who was not a very fast walker, began slowing us down. Henry wanted to send her back to the farm, accompanied by Geraldine, but he was eventually persuaded to give her a piggyback ride instead; thus, Doris could remain with her sister that little bit longer.

The journey was rather quiet – my young companions seemed subdued by the day's events. Doris often had a blank stare, and Geraldine was becoming unusually withdrawn as well. Fortunately, Henry was a bit of a character. He soon perked us all up by telling us amusing stories about when he worked on a farm as a young man or he just kept our minds occupied by asking us about the homes that we had originally come from.

After about an hour, we made it to the station, where Henry – to his relief – was finally able to put Doris down. I bought the one-way ticket, and then went with my companions to the platform to wait patiently for the train. I was told that it was due in an hour or so. That surprised me, as I had been woken up particularly early that morning in order to ensure that I would not miss it. It seemed that I had rushed and missed a lot of sleep unnecessarily but I could do nothing about it now. Anyway, I thought, I could always have a bit of a doze on the long ride home.

As we sat on the platform benches, Doris and I exchanged our final pieces of advice to each other. Knowing that she would be starting to go to school within the next year or so, I told her to be a good pupil and do well there, while she told me to remember to get off the train at the right stop – and not to be a silly girl!

"I'll write to you when I get home," I said and she said that she would stay in touch as well.

We three girls then spent the rest of the time reminiscing about the various adventures that we had had since the evacuation, especially the good times on the farm or at school. Henry interrupted at one point, saying that he thought that he should get back to the farm to carry on with his work and obviously take Doris and Geraldine with him, but they helped me to persuade him to wait a little longer.

Fortunately for Henry, the train to take me away turned up about ten minutes later. When I first saw its tiny shape appear in the distance, I started to get butterflies in my stomach. I left it to Henry to herald its arrival. As it slowly neared the platform, it loomed large and screeched its presence.

Just before it came to a halt, I turned to Doris and gave her most of the money that I had left in my purse. I no longer had a need for it, as I knew that I was to be home in a few hours – assuming that I would get out at the right station, of course, and not have to buy any more train tickets! Doris, though, would now have to survive a lot longer away from home than I would. Hers – I recognised – was the greater need now. I kissed her goodbye on the cheek and left her with a big sisterly hug.

"Goodbye, Lily," she said.

"Goodbye, Doris," I replied. "You look after yourself. Keep in touch, now. I'll see you again soon."

I then gave Geraldine a hug, saying, "I hope everything works out all right for you too, in the end."

To the pair of them I added, "And you're both going to look after each other, all right?" to which they replied – in unison – "Yes."

Then I thanked Henry for looking after me.

"Now, Lilian, you make sure you have a safe journey, mind..." he said, "... and don't forget your stop!" he added, reiterating the wise advice of Doris'.

Only a few people got out of the train and only a few got in. I was the last of those to climb aboard. Henry passed me my bag and gas mask, and closed the door behind me. My companions all stood only a few feet away. The sight of my sad young sister transfixed me. My mother had told me to stand by her but now my actions were leaving her more alone than she had ever been.

"Will you come and visit us?" Doris asked, dejectedly.

I had previously told her that my journey was definitely one-way only and – with heart-breaking sincerity – stated the same again: "No, Doris. I'm going home to stay. I won't be coming back."

I wanted to grab Doris there and then and take her with me; it seemed so easy. The practical limitations meant that I really could not.

Then the whistle sounded, announcing the end of the train's temporary pause. Racing metal wheels screeched as they slid on the hard tracks and then took a steady grip. The unstoppable, poignant momentum began pulling me away, to begin the journey home.

"Goodbye, Doris," I said one last time and Doris replied,

"Goodbye, Lily," one last time. She tried to smile and look happy for me but her face expressed everything that the young child felt as her only relative was leaving her behind to fend for herself.

Henry, who had rested his comforting, firm hands on the shoulders of Doris and Geraldine for a moment, now prompted Doris to raise her arm up and then she, followed by Geraldine and then Henry, began waving to me. I waved back and continued doing so until, with the growing distance between us, I could make them out no more. Then, emotionally exhausted, I slowly sat down in my carriage.

I stared blankly at the passing scenery as I shed more tears for my little sister. I closed my eyes to see her face again, to

see her running excitedly towards me; I heard her laugh with me. On the journey, I was taking with me a dear collection of memories. It was as though her spirit was going home with me. Then the train suddenly jolted, my eyes opened and I reminded myself that I had just left the individual behind.

I wondered how long the war would go on – how long it would be before all of the displaced could return home. I felt that it had not been a good way to leave a vulnerable sister. The butterflies in my stomach were ever present and I tried to relax on the long journey and remember the advice that I was given – not to forget my stop – but I also had a lot of time to think about many other things before I got home. I was to be quite emotionally drained by the time I eventually arrived.

7

Home... for a while

Arriving back home

BY THE MIDDLE of the afternoon, my slow, clattering train swayed and meandered its way into my old London station (where I did not forget to get off!). I collected my bag and gas mask, carefully alighted and then left the concourse.

I stood for a moment, acclimatising myself to the old 'feel' of the bustling metropolitan environment – one devoid of the sounds of rural animals but with plenty of new barrage balloons flying over its open spaces.

I was surprised at how many children were present on the streets; many of whom could have been evacuees who had returned, while others might not have even been evacuated in the first place. I had imagined that I would be the only child walking around London after leaving her billet and that all of the judgmental adults I would pass on my way home, would be hostile and pointing and staring at me... *"Look! There's Lilian. Quick, everyone – point and stare at her. She's the only child in the whole of Great Britain who's going back home before the end of the war. Boo! Boo!"*

However, no one pointed or stared at me; nothing was said.

When I got home, my mother – who had been expecting me – was very welcoming. Almost straight away, I was given a refreshing cup of tea, and began debriefing her as to all that had happened to Doris and me while we had been away. As we sat and spoke at length to each other, I realised that

I was experiencing something that I had been missing for a long time: I was conversing with an adult who had a friendly ear for me. I had almost forgotten how pleasant it was to be in the presence of one so sympathetic, whose attentiveness could so unburden my troubled mind.

Early that evening I wrote Doris a letter, just as I said I would, telling her that I had arrived home safely and letting her know that her mother was still thinking of her every day. I reminded her that whenever she next wanted to tell us anything, she only had to write to us. I included with my letter a stamped, addressed envelope for her to use. I could do no more than that for Doris.

Afterwards, I went to my bedroom and occupied it now as a solitary child. I lay on my bed and looked across at Doris' empty one. The space was quiet, almost deafeningly so, yet this rather shattered girl managed to fall asleep despite it, to the imagined sound of the girl who was no longer there. A few hours later, I would be awoken for a very late dinner. It had been a long and stressful day.

The next day, I posted my letter to Doris and then went looking for my old friend, Jeanette, but she had remained in her billet; she had not returned. Nevertheless, I had other friends to go out with. Many had been in London very early in the war, when it was initially hard to find other children to play with; however, that problem resolved itself, as perhaps half of all evacuees were now back home.

Father... yet again!
For what appeared to be the final time, my father returned to the house and then left again shortly afterwards, taking away a compliant Rhona to live with him. Rhona was the one child of his whom he actually liked and was the only one of his offspring who liked him in return. Her leaving us was not a disappointment to me; I had little to miss.

Trying out the mansion – evacuation number two
My mother did not send me back to school. In fact, I do not know if the establishment was even functioning as a school any more – many civil buildings, by this time, had been taken over by the authorities for war-related purposes. Then, one day, my mother's relaxed attitude to my education became clear when I was told to prepare for a second evacuation, this time with her accompanying me.

As usual, my mother went to her mother – who conveniently lived just around the corner – and deposited my young sister, Nancy, with her. Normally, the baby-sitting would only be for the few hours while my mother was at work but now it seemed that it was to be for an indeterminate period.

When all was ready, we took our rather long railway journey out to the country and then stood in awe at the impressive and domineering sight of our destination – a magnificent white mansion. Sandwiching its long driveway were two massive lawns with large trees around the edges. Smaller trees occupied occasional solitary spots where the rolling stretches of greenery dipped a little, giving the whole 'sea' of grass a less regular, and more three-dimensional, appearance.

Unfortunately, appearances were deceptive, for the large, cold hall that we were meant to sleep in was empty except for a couple of rudimentary mattresses that were lying on the uncarpeted floor. The demeaning 'accommodation' looked as though it had been left unused for years. It was immediately encouraging us to leave, which we did the next day.

The shelter
In the local streets, swarms of builders were busily constructing several large, single-storey brick buildings, one every fifty yards or so, for people like us – those with no Anderson shelter because they had no garden in which to put it.

After my friend Jeanette returned home, she and I became friendly with two local boys. When a small air-raid shelter was completed outside the brewery, the boys suggested that I should explore it with them.

I approached and then cautiously entered the building, which was clearly meant for more than one family. For their sleeping arrangements, several wooden bunks had been built around the sides. I went up to one and sat on it. Suddenly, the boys turned the lights out, ran outside and then closed the door. I immediately found myself alone in the darkness and quite disorientated.

"Let me out!" I called. "Turn on the lights!"

They giggled until I became hysterical.

"Wait till I get out!" I yelled, deciding to change my approach from pleading to threatening. To this, my gaolers finally relented; they opened the door. As I stepped back into the bright daylight again and looked at the pair of them, I could not help thinking how childish they were. I decided that I would definitely be seeing them less often in future.

The enemy now just across the Channel

On the 10th of May 1940, the war that had seemed so 'phoney' for so long suddenly became much more real: German troops began their blitzkrieg – their offensive in the west. It was an unhappy coincidence for Winston Churchill, who became our Prime Minister that same day.

The Germans began by simply marching around a major – but incomplete – allied defensive construction, called the Maginot Line, and quickly swallowed up the countries of Luxembourg, Holland and Belgium.

The name of Dunkirk, in France, was given great prominence on the radio for several days around the end of May, as was the fate of the Royal Navy. Much of our army was brought back from that port, back to Blighty. It spoke well of the Allied will to resist that so many gallantly gave their lives to enable so many others to escape and continue the fight. Reports from Dunkirk ceased in early June.

Important rivers, towns and ports briefly held prominence in the news. Each was defended with apparently increasing fanaticism by our heroic armed forces; each was systematically lost to the Nazis – the self-proclaimed (so-called) 'master race'. Hitler's advancing army was beginning to appear quite unstoppable. Soon, all utterances from a free France were silenced. About six weeks after the start of their attack, the Nazis had subjugated around a hundred million more souls. Now, no country in Europe was still resisting the Germans – except for Great Britain.

No confident remarks from my mother could disguise the fact that the outlook for my nation – and us – did not appear too good. Only a modest area of countryside and some twenty-one miles of sea to the south now separated us from the ruthless Hun.

At that low point, Mr Churchill displayed true qualities of leadership by giving the most inspiring speeches of exhortation over the radio. His fighting sentiments gave my mother and me – and many others – courage and confidence. We were not going to 'go down', as they say, without a fight. He made it clear that all of Britain was to be the next battleground. My compatriots were encouraged never to surrender but to maintain their heroic struggle from the first enemy landing grounds to the envisioned final redoubt upon the last defiant hill. Any invading Germans were to be engaged fanatically – and to the death! Churchill's rhetoric steeled everyone's hearts for the testing times ahead although, possibly justifiably, he did seem to frighten the life out of us just beforehand!

In that air of defiance – and virtual desperation – a volunteer army of citizens was formed: the Local Defence Volunteers (the LDVs). Any man who could walk and carry something lethal – even if it was only as simple as a broom handle with a knife attached to the end of it – was eligible to join. The inexperienced LDVs appeared the equal of the most hardened Nazi as they practised bayonet charges using their home-made spears against hanging stuffed sacks... but I doubted that their real enemy would be so accommodating as to hang around while he was being stabbed to death. The mission of our part-time army – of village butchers, bakers and candlestick makers... and the like – although glorious in its inception, had something of the suicidal in its execution.

Together with a few foreign survivors from earlier battles against the Germans, and some spirited volunteers from far away, overseas, our armed forces now stood waiting expectantly in the eye of the storm and braced themselves for the inevitable onslaught.

For the millions living under the Nazi jackboot, our victory in the coming battle could give hope – that their day of deliverance would still come. With our ascendancy over our very right to exist, friendly neutral nations could be encouraged to take up arms with us in the living noble cause of liberty; when, until now, they had seemed content only to watch from a safe distance as all of humanity around them was dying.

Even as nation after nation was falling to the agents of nihilism, the failing spirit of this island race was, yet, heartened by one who instilled in all of us confidence, hope and the will to endure, to resist... to prevail!

And when the fine words were spoken – in that pensive, determined tone – of civilisation approaching its greatest epoch, our nation took courage in its moment of decision and prepared to behold the destiny that would decide all.

8

Now farther than ever before

Leaving home... one more time

MY MOTHER GOT me up unusually early one morning. A nice warm breakfast was waiting for me but when I had finished it and carried out my usual ablutions, she abruptly came up and prepared me to go on what appeared to be some sort of journey.

"Are we going somewhere?" I asked as my mother proceeded to put an outdoor coat, scarf and a pair of gloves on me.

"Why are we hurrying?" I protested as she grabbed a suitcase of my belongings that she had just packed. I felt her hand grip mine tightly. She then sped down the stairs, closely towing me along in her wake. As we both stepped into the cold morning air, I turned to see the door to my home being firmly closed behind me.

Where was I going, I asked myself.

There was urgency in her movement. We hurried past familiar old, small buildings and several streets of north London. As we approached the local railway station that I had visited twice before in recent months, I realised that I was probably being taken to start yet another long journey, in which case my day of travelling had only just begun!

"Why are we here?" I asked, looking at my mother's tense, white face.

By now, I was not expecting a response and I was not surprised that none was forthcoming but it was entirely out of character for my mother to remain so silent. She was never normally one to be lost for words. I sensed that she was very unhappy about something, as though she was full of resolve to complete an unpleasant mission of some sort although, on reflection, I was not too enamoured about the way the day had been progressing so far either.

The station was crowded and full of bustle. I had a label pinned on me with my personal details written on it and the small suitcase was put into my hand. Before I realised it, I was being thrust into a carriage.

I tried to rationalize the morning's events, to pause – if I could – and take stock of the situation. I became aware that I was by myself on a long seat, opposite a solitary woman. Beside me was the carriage window through which I stared with a sense of incredulity at my subdued mother. She was standing outside on the platform and leaving me to be conveyed alone to a mysterious destination (at least it was mysterious to me – I was just hoping that it was not for her as well!).

Fear gripped me as I gazed into my mother's misty eyes. The more obscured by sadness they became, the clearer they betrayed the purpose of my journey out of the city. I felt the pain and anguish shown in her face. I knew that I had to be brave, stoically sit back and just accept what was happening.

"Would you tell my daughter when to get off, please?" my mother asked the other passenger.

"Where is she going to?" said the woman, startled to find herself suddenly becoming a party to my evacuation.

"To Tenby," was the spluttered reply.

"I'll do that," the woman replied and, sensing a tense situation, added in a friendly manner, "I'll see she's all right. Don't worry." The lady nodded and smiled at me.

Suddenly, a whistle blew and the door of the carriage was closed.

My mother made a hurried remark to reassure me: "The lady will tell you when you're to get off."

The words trailed as the almost deafening sound of the train started. As it gathered speed, my mother waved, and as her diminutive figure faded into the distance, I had a sudden feeling of complete desolation. For a third time in only a few months, I found myself heading to an unknown place, an indefinite number of miles away.

"Are we there yet?" I asked the woman after we had gone a short distance.

"No. Don't worry. I'll tell you when we are."

I looked out of the carriage window and saw the now-familiar passing scenery of fields and isolated houses. I tried to remain positive and attentive to the changing views but I quickly lost all interest in them. I felt abandoned.

Why was this happening to me, I asked myself over and over. It was the longest journey that I had ever taken and it was probably made to seem even more extensive than it actually was because I had no idea when it would end.

I looked at the lady opposite many times, wondering if she had forgotten to tell me that I had arrived at my destination. She looked composed and self-assured, and she did not appear to have forgotten me. She had a pleasant manner, although she rarely spoke. Her short, wavy black hair – streaked with grey – framed her middle-aged face. Because of her demeanour and dark apparel, I assumed that she enjoyed a typical middle-class lifestyle and was, perhaps, a teacher. She certainly seemed to have the required responsible attitude (at least, I assumed that she had such a responsible attitude; after all, she had not yet told me when to get off!).

New beginnings
After several interminable hours, we drew into a very small station – one that was much less substantial than the one that I had just left. There were very few people around.

Suddenly, the lady opposite spoke: "You're in Tenby. Take your case. Someone will be meeting you…"

The rest of the sentence went unheard amidst a sudden burst of activity. A door slammed and I walked slowly and apprehensively along the platform. After I had walked to the end of it, I stopped and put my case down. No one was there to meet me!

I was alone and quickly felt panic-stricken. I looked around at my new, strange environment and tried to make sense of what had happened to me – at least, of where I was. Rolling hills were all around in the distance and, before them, there was a considerable countryside. The railway station 'island' was in the middle of that; upon it, my solitary, little figure stood virtually lost. I could not be sure how far I had travelled that day but it was clear that I had left my city life far behind. Several minutes passed and I became increasingly apprehensive. Suddenly, the figure of a girl greeted me.

"Hello!" she said in a strange accent, the like of which I had never heard before and which, I surmised, I would quickly have to get used to.

"I'm sorry I'm a bit late. I see you're the girl from London," she added, glancing at the label pinned to my coat.

She then grabbed my arm – the same one by which my mother had earlier pulled me along – and proceeded to rush out of the station with me in her desperate tow. I began to worry that everywhere I was to go might be in a state of immediacy and that my poor little, over-tugged appendage might finish the day being somewhat longer, and consequently more conspicuous, than it had been at the start… *"Ah, so you must be Lilian. My, what a long arm you have!"*

Pausing outside, she told me that her name was Gly. Ahead lay a long, steep hill, which I viewed with dismay.

She noted my expression and remarked, "You'll soon get used to it," before commencing to escort me up it.

Being tired after the journey, I did not pay much attention to the hill that we climbed or the streets that we passed. However, when we stopped, I looked around and was astounded to see that I was before a great castle wall – an impressive dominating presence of ancient grey stones and arches.

My thoughts were abruptly interrupted by the loud remark from Gly: "We're here!"

I stared in front of me with eyebrows raised. We were standing in front of a large porch with coloured tiles. The brass step gleamed, as did the large handle and letter box on the heavy wooden door. To the left was the huge window of a shop. Long glass shelves were lined with necklaces, leather purses and gloves, embroidered items, skeins of wool and other fancy items.

"Do you live *here*?" I ventured.

"Of course," was the curt reply from one surprised that I should have asked such a question.

As the door opened into a wide passage, I immediately viewed two rather short, mature ladies standing there. One had silver hair, which was pulled back into the shape of a bun. She introduced herself as Mrs Morgan and, turning to the other lady with darker hair, indicated that she was her unmarried sister, Miss Dickinson, who lived with her and her husband. They wore nearly ankle-length crepe dresses of dark colours with a square of white lace inserted in the low neckline.

I turned to my companion, to observe her at close quarters. She was a few years older than I was. Her hair was medium brown with tussled waves and curls. Her eyes were blue and her cheeks, rosy.

"Come downstairs!" she called to me.

I left my belongings and followed her to the end of the passage and down a flight of narrow stairs. At the bottom was a sharp corner that opened into a larder. At right angles lay the entrance to the large kitchen. As I entered, I could see several silver-coloured metal bells arranged in line, just below the ceiling.

"They are to summon the servants upstairs to various rooms," was the statement made as I gazed at them.

On the left was a wooden table, almost the length of the room, which was scrubbed nearly white. This was to be where I was to sit for meals with the family. I was given the doorway seat, while Mrs Morgan had a seat adjacent to the fire.

Another smaller table was placed opposite, in front of a large window. This was for the use of the two maids and the nanny; the latter fed and looked after Mrs Morgan's youngest child – a baby with curly, fair hair. I was surprised to learn that Mrs Morgan was indeed the mother, for she appeared beyond the typical child-rearing age.

As well as this child, she had a daughter, Gly (the girl who had met me), and two sons. The eldest, Idris, was at university, training to be a dentist. The other, Alun – who was of a similar age to mine – was at boarding school. Both of the boys, like their siblings, had curly hair.

Also in the kitchen, facing the table, was a very large wooden dresser – indeed, the largest that I had ever seen. The shelves were crammed with plates of all sizes, cups and china serving dishes. Above the large, black fire range, which incidentally incorporated a small oven next to a fire, were several silver tureens.

The remaining wall, alongside the large table, was lined with narrow drawers. These held sets of silver cutlery, including a fish set. These were cleaned with silver polish and then washed. Sometimes one of the maids did this, although, later, the other evacuees and I did this chore. At the beginning, there was just one other evacuee – a girl called Rosa. Later, her two sisters and my younger sister, Nancy, would join us.

Off the kitchen, lay the scullery. It was large and daunting, with a grey concrete floor and bare walls with a few makeshift wooden shelves. There was a huge enamel sink with a long draining area. I was to learn that this was necessary for the large amount of utensils used.

A maid called Ada usually did the washing-up. Her small bedroom, on the top floor, was next to mine. It was furnished with a bowl and jug on a stand, a dark-oak chest of drawers and a bed. My room was larger and contained four beds. One was a 'double', which Rosa and eventually her sister, Margaret (also known as 'Maggie'), slept in. A double wardrobe, small dressing table and one chest of drawers were available for our use. The other bedroom on this floor was Miss Dickinson's.

After seeing the kitchen, I was invited to unpack my clothes. I decided to just take what I wanted from my suitcase and get organised the next day. I felt tired, and awaited with trepidation the new life of mine that was about to begin.

9

My new home, town, family and friends

The new girl about town
(Dramatization)

THE NEXT DAY, Gly showed me around my new home town. As we left the house, the imposing grey, mediaeval gate and walls directly outside once more immediately dwarfed me. Presumably, they had long ago stood to keep the unwelcome visitor out. Now, I almost sensed that their purpose had changed: to keep this involuntary visitor in.

Leaving them behind, we strolled along short, narrow, cobbled streets of shops and houses, and long, quiet, dark alleyways where strange ancient buildings hid. Streaks of broad, lingering shadows punctuated the bright shafts of a blinding sunlight. A large church stood a short distance away, near groups of demure tall, old, pale-coloured buildings, huddled together as though for mutual support.

Beyond them lay a scene of majestic magnificence – a rippling, turquoise, limitless sea. A golden, sandy beach – scratched by 'necklaces' of anti-invasion barbed wire – defied the crashing, white surf. This was my first trip to the coast, a seemingly magical place where the land ended and infinite water began. I stared at the undulating, glassy blue and the distant horizon. Such a view I had never seen before – the edge of my new world.

"Lilian, Lilian!" it cried. "Come and play, for all around is your new playground."

I responded to my new playmate with a clearly audible, "Oh, yes."

"Do you like where you're living, Lilian?" Gly asked.

I just nodded and took in the scenery.

"Shall we explore some more?" asked Gly.

"Explore some *more?*" I responded, incredulous to learn that there was even more than the ocean's inspiring shoreline below to discover.

Gly took me along the grassy clifftop, where I began to pass along ruined walls and beneath the partial remains of the battlements of Tenby's castle. The collection of roughly hewn stones and mediaeval cement remained defiantly holding itself together despite hundreds of years of the wearying effects of the elements and the destructive hand of man. Arrow slits drew me towards them, to view the once-contested ground below. Murderous arrows surely flew from there to find their mortal mark, to cut their luckless attacking foes down.

I passed beneath great arches and scrambled around square towers. I climbed numerous stone steps that betrayed the wear of centuries in their curved, misshapen forms and looked out of the fragments of shattered windows. I balanced on a flimsy ledge and spied a glimpse of the land beyond, the fine dominion of the Tenby ancestors. I had reached the high realm of the knights of antiquity and their fair ladies, and reflected upon a past now long decayed.

When Gly called out to me, I carefully descended the structure and returned to her. In her eyes I saw a certain civic pride, born perhaps from a lifetime spent in close proximity to the great monuments, the heritage of a once-glorious nobility.

I began to wonder if I should have been so quick to tread all over the ruins with such a display of happy abandon.

Gly did not reproach me for my carefree escapade, which could hardly have caused any more damage to the ancient structures. In future, however, I desisted from climbing over anything else that looked interesting unless my somewhat austere guide first gave me some sign of her approval.

At the quay, many boats lay abandoned on the sand like stranded whales. They could not be taken to sea during wartime in case the Germans attacked them. When I asked how the boats were able to be so far from the water, Gly tried explaining how the sea comes and goes.

"That's called the tide," she said, and then she described how the sun and the moon – pulling the sea 'up and down' – made the tide go out and come in, not only in Tenby but also at every other coastline around the world.

"Which bit's the tide?" I asked, looking out at the water – eager to observe it going up and down, and in and out.

"The tide is all of the sea – when it moves in and out. You've always got to make sure you never get cut off by the tide, Lilian, if you're ever down on the beach. It can come in very quickly... before you're even aware of it!" warned a concerned, protective Gly.

We continued along the sandy edge of the quay and ascended the adjacent hill. I was immediately lost to the attractive view of the quaint harbour as I sat down and found myself lost in vast fields of brightly coloured, wild blooms that completely carpeted the surrounding clifftops.

"Would you like to go for a swim, sometime?" Gly asked.

"Yes," I said, without a moment's hesitation.

"We can go, if you like, when my brothers are all back on their holidays."

"All right," I replied, looking forward to a bit of a paddle later.

Returning home after about an hour, I was dwarfed once more beside the town's massive mediaeval gate and walls.

"They go right around the town... almost. Tourists come

to see them..." Gly proudly declared of the monumental masonry. She stopped suddenly and corrected herself: "... used to come to see them – before the war."

She spoke as though she was proud that she lived within the outskirts of a castle when not everyone could do so. I felt like saying something equally impressive about my Weston Rise area of London but the view from my old doorway was as nothing compared to that magnificent achievement of the early industrious folk of Tenby.

The growing 'family'

Life in Tenby was pleasant and the routine, predictable. I had a sense of security now, which made quite a welcome change after the chaotic upheavals over the previous few weeks.

Rosa was in similar circumstances to mine and that encouraged us to develop a close bond of friendship. We gave each other mutual support as we made the rapid and profound adjustments that were so incumbent upon us as evacuees.

The Morgans tried to help us to become acclimatized to our new surroundings. They encouraged us to treat them as our family – to make us feel at home – so we called them 'Mummy' and 'Dad'. Miss Dickinson became 'Auntie'.

Each night, we kissed Mrs Morgan on the cheek when saying goodnight and, overall, I soon began to feel as though I was living with some sympathetic, understanding, well-to-do relatives – albeit very distant ones whom I had never seen before.

Mr Morgan and my new school

Mr Morgan was a soldier in the Great War of 1914 to 1918. The house in which we were now living, which used to belong to Mrs Morgan's parents, was originally his billet. He eventually married Mrs Morgan and stayed in the home.

Unfortunately, there was less affection between him

and his sister-in-law, Miss Dickinson. I heard many of the constant arguments between the pair of them, although these altercations did not really affect me and I learned to keep a low profile whenever their voices began to be raised.

It had been decided that I was to attend Tenby Council School, the local junior school, which was only a few hundred yards away. Mr Morgan was its headmaster. The journey to school with him was one of awe, as nearly everyone acknowledged him and showed him great reverence.

All of the way down the street, people would say greetings like, "Good morning, Mr Morgan," or "Hello, Mr Morgan. How are you?"

You felt that he was an important personage and held in high regard. Similarly, I felt privileged just to be in his company. Mr Morgan was amiable to everyone. He knew no barriers and was happy to talk to anyone of any background, regardless of the consequences. Once, he had a conversation with a tramp who happened to be passing through Tenby and who had stopped for a while to sit on a bench that was located opposite the house.

Miss Dickinson did not hold quite the same disregard for social situations. She reprimanded her brother-in-law for talking to the tramp. By way of explanation, Mr Morgan said that he was interested in the person's life story and what it was that had brought about their unfortunate dire circumstances.

Mr Morgan's noble attributes came to the attention of others in the town. They held him in such high regard that they offered him the post of town mayor. He declined it, though, explaining that he would not have had the time for such a duty. Instead, he preferred to devote himself to all of the many children for whom he cared.

Around a hundred pupils attended my school. Unfortunately, I broke a rule there on one occasion and was consequently sent to Mr Morgan's office to be caned. When

I went there, I explained what I had done and he warned me not to do it again but he looked upon me kindly – he would not cane me for my misdemeanour. Instead, he kept me waiting in the office for a few minutes, to make it appear as though I was being punished, and then he allowed me to return to my class. He told me to behave as though I had just been caned.

When I re-entered the classroom and sat down, I groaned while giving due respect to a bottom apparently well chastised. The prospect of receiving a real flogging, if my delivery was anything less than perfect, kept my demeanour constant and believable. Consequently, I received no well-deserved accolade for a sterling piece of child acting that day but, fortunately, I got no caning either!

Towards the end of term, lessons started to give way to less academic exercises. I took part in a fancy-dress parade of 'Eastern' costumes in front of the rest of the school and I also became very much involved in organising a *Cinderella* show. I felt that the play went well and I was complimented on my central performance. At the end of the day, we just had a bit of fun, which happily marked the completion of what had proven to be, for many of us, quite a strenuous academic year.

Miss Dickinson

I should not forget to mention Miss Dickinson. She had been a Quaker missionary in Africa, and returned from the mysterious continent with plenty of souvenirs, which she displayed in her bedroom. They were crammed into every inch of space – from the ceiling to the floor. Also scattered around the room were books, paintings and bundles of wool. The paintings were excellent renditions of hers. They were mostly scenic and encapsulated the beauty of such natural creations as Tenby's beach and interesting rock formations nearby.

When she wanted to do another picture, she would diligently carry her paints and easel to her chosen spot very early in the morning – when it was quiet and few people would be about. There she would spend all of her time carefully doing justice to the wonderful local vistas. She displayed the finished results throughout the house, with the staircase, in particular, being used for several of them.

When I was in the house and the beautiful scenery outside was hidden from my view, I was always reminded of it through being surrounded by so many of Miss Dickinson's striking works of art. They seemed so real and engaging that they often drew me into the 'other world' of the canvas – a seascape for instance.

Sometimes, I would almost find myself standing on that battered beach, looking up at the soaring seagulls and hearing their squawks amidst the terrifying crash of giant, white waves upon the nearby jagged, grey rocks. Upon my face, I would feel a gentle, fine spray – particles of the shattered, breaking surf being carried on a raw, mercurial wind.

The paintings were the 'perfect' creations that dominated the 'imperfect' world in which they were displayed. The places that Miss Dickinson depicted, whether tempestuous or serene, were so enchanting and far removed from the troubles of the day that they easily just took me away.

10

Start of the summer holidays

(Improvised dialogue)

The great expedition

AT THE START of my summer holidays, in perfect weather and with supplies of sandwiches and little home-made pies for lunch, and a bottle of drinking water, Gly, Alun and Idris led Rosa and me to explore places beyond the town that we had previously never been to.

Rosa and I were shown 'sand-wormy-things' and then a rock-pool of indolent starfish.

"Come on!" I urged but the little creatures remained motionless at the bottom of their little watery world of lethargy.

I got a small piece of wood and gently pushed it against one of them but it just slid off the rock and then slowly wriggled away, beneath another rock.

"Boo!" said Rosa – a sentiment that was quickly echoed by the young, attentive audience. "Buck your ideas up or we won't come and see you any more."

Disappointed, Gly and her brothers left the rock pool behind and continued along the beach while Rosa and I took our shoes and socks off, and shadowed them from within the edge of the alluring, beautiful blue ocean, which was now only a short way off.

The climb

After a while, although Rosa and I remained just within reach of the surf, we were definitely getting closer to the cliffs. When the encroaching sea began consuming what remained of the beach, and everyone was left standing virtually right next to each other, I found myself presented with an interesting problem and I very much looked forward to discovering the Morgans' solution to it.

"Are we going back now?" Rosa asked, so optimistically.

"The tide's coming in everywhere," Idris said. "If we try to go back now, we'll be just as cut off in a few minutes."

Then Alun enthusiastically added, "It's got dangerous currents. If we try swimming through it, we could all drown!"

"I want to go home!" I said, anxiously.

"Don't worry, you two," said Gly, standing noticeably taller than her two small charges: Rosa and me (or 'the short people', as I feared we would always be remembered).

"The only way out, I think, ladies and gentlemen... is up," Idris declared, pointing up at the impressive cliff beside us.

"Up *there*?" Rosa exclaimed, shocked at the frightening towering source of her supposed deliverance.

I looked up and contemplated the climb; it clearly appeared far harder than the ascent of a gas lamp, something that I would have been confident of achieving. Had there been such a device, I might have considered climbing up that and hanging around on top of it until the tide had receded, when I could have come down again. Had there been several up and down the beaches, we could all have climbed up them and hung around for a few hours. They could have been the means of saving five lives. Now, we were liable to pay the ultimate price for such an absence. Obviously, the local authorities had not considered it important enough to equip the beaches with such potential life-savers. Oh, what a cruel short-sighted world it was turning out to be!

"Follow me," Idris commanded confidently as he proceeded to grab what he could of the almost vertical side of the grey and brown cliff, and ascend as though he had done it a hundred times before.

Rosa and I first brushed as much sticky sand as we could off our irritatingly dirty, damp feet and then forced them into our lovely clean, dry shoes, for an itchy feeling that was not to be the most pleasant experience of the day. Alun now started the climb. Then Gly told me to go next and follow the same course that the boys had just taken. I grabbed hold of some useful plants and rocks that were serendipitously sticking out of the cliff and made my way up the thirty feet or so of the escape route. I reached the top without any serious mishap – fortunately! Rosa pulled herself up after me.

Gly then followed along, at the rear. She tried to ensure that we all climbed carefully and she gave us constant words of encouragement like: "That's it girls. Keep going."

I found those far more welcome than the negative ones of Alun's such as: "If you fall off the cliff, you could get killed!" At the top, we rested a while before recommencing the expedition.

Suddenly, thousands of tall trees unexpectedly surrounded us (although not in a 'surreal subversive-pine-larch-tree-collective ambush' sort of way). We had actually entered a dense wood that impeded our advance along the gently undulating cliff but we continued, nevertheless.

The journey along the cliff top was uphill. Every few minutes, we gingerly – if foolishly – approached the cliff's edge to check how high we now were.

"Don't go too far, Lily," Idris once warned me as I attempted to observe our situation without taking enough care.

At another time, though, my curiosity got the better of me. I wanted to see beyond the edge of the cliff but the ground towards it was sloping quite severely, so I laid myself down on the ground and crept along on my stomach for the last few feet.

When I reached the end, I stretched my neck and glimpsed the sea far below. Every sight that had befallen me until now had always been more dramatic than the previous. This was no exception but the scene was enhanced this time by viewing it from such a precarious position. I was a hundred or more feet up and looking down on massive, smooth-sided, grey cliffs. If an advancing tide had earlier trapped us on the beach below, then the sheer, vast, uncompromising barrier of stone at our backs would certainly have offered no escape: it was impossible to scale.

The Morgans' children possibly knew that about this area of the coast. The journey so far seemed to attest to their being experienced masters of it. They knew how to harvest the visions of wild beauty; how to challenge inexorable tides fearlessly; and to keep in their 'pockets of knowledge' – for emergencies – a ready supply of hair-raising last-minute, cliff-based routes to salvation.

The real master of all that I surveyed, though, must surely have been the sea. It was a relentless force of nature, forever striking at the base of the cliffs – battering the lines of defiant, jagged rocks in front of them – and grasping at all within its greedy reach. The crashing of the white waves far below was barely audible above the sound of the chilly salt-air whistling past me. Indefatigable gusts of wind – coming unhindered from across the ocean – were directed up against the side of the promontory. They blasted my face and blew my hair back. I had never experienced anywhere like it before in my life. I lay transfixed by the awe-inspiring spectacle of a monumental nature. I hung on for dear life to my grassy, sloping, precarious edge of oblivion.

"Come on, Lily. We're going now," Gly called out from some distance away as she and the others began walking off.

She brought me back to a sense of reality. Forgetting

about the scene below me, I began concentrating instead on trying to get back up the slope and away from the end of the cliff. Fortunately, my piece of it had remained firm and had not collapsed into the sea, which was something that I had always slightly feared. However, I now began to realise just how slippery it was. I was finding it difficult to slide backwards, up such a slope – a predicament that I had not anticipated when I had been easily sliding down it. I tried clasping tightly at clumps of grass while pushing with my arms, to try to move backwards. However, I only managed to move back a foot or so before some grass – which I had just taken hold of – suddenly came away in my hand.

I let out a desperate cry, "Oo, er!" and quickly lay flat. Fortunately, my instinctive reaction immediately increased my body's traction on the grassy surface, which prevented me sliding any further forwards.

"Are you coming, Lily?" Idris called out.

"Yes!" I replied, before I quietly added to myself, "Or going – one way or the other."

I eventually made much steadier progress when I moved more slowly while shifting my weight from side to side. When there was sufficient room and the ground was much more level, I was able to stand up and walk the rest of the way back into the woods.

After I rejoined the group, Idris remarked, "You were hanging around a lot back there," as though 'hanging around' was no longer considered a useful ability. To me, it was something to be whole-heartedly cherished, unlike that 'sliding off' thing that had just seemed ever so much easier to accomplish.

"I couldn't get back up the slope," I explained, expecting them all to understand that, minutes before, I had only just managed to stop myself sliding off the cliff and into the sea. However, that did not seem to mean much to most of them. Rosa showed a little interest, though, so I recounted my sorry

133

story to her, after which she began recounting her sorry story to me – of how she had acquired all of her many wounds while climbing around in the woods.

After a while, we all began emerging into a clearing, where the land started falling quite steeply towards sea level, as did we! A cascade of clear water appeared and we raced towards it.

'That looks very nice,' and then 'I'm getting quite bored with it now' I *almost* felt like saying as my companions and I involuntarily ran straight past. We finally landed, with considerable speed, on an expanse of welcome soft sand.

The cave

When we were ready, we carried on until we stood beside an apparently innocuous cave with a tall, inviting entrance.

"Did you want to have a look in there?" Idris asked.

"Why? What's in it?" I replied.

"You'll find out if you go in," said Gly, tantalizingly.

Then Alun gleefully added, "A long-dead pirate."

I initially suspected that the cave contained the remains of an impressively tall buccaneer. It soon dawned on me, though, that 'long-dead' did not refer to the corpse's noteworthy overall length but actually described the amount of time that the sailor had lain expired.

"He clambered up this, here, ragged coast a hundred years ago after his galleon was wrecked in a great, frightening storm out there..." Alun explained, pointing at the sea, appropriately, "... and he took shelter in this cave, where his strength finally gave out and he died."

He then illustrated the historical event with some amateur dramatics involving desperately crawling along on the sand and gasping.

"His body's been in there ever since," he added, confidently.

I pondered for a few seconds what I had just been told

and then, being more than a little sceptical, enquired, "How do you know all that, then?"

"It's all part of the legend around here," Idris said.

"What legend?" asked Rosa.

"The legend of the long-dead pirate," was Idris' not entirely unexpected response.

Then Gly added, "It's also said that he had some treasure with him that he took from his ship before it went down but no one's ever had the courage to go into the cave to have a look for it."

"Well, let's do it now, then!" Rosa bravely ventured as she cautiously approached its high entrance. She hesitated upon reaching it and stared intensely into the darkness. Curiosity drew me close behind her.

Alun followed, remarking, "The first things you'll notice when you go in there will probably be his white teeth."

"Why – did he drop them on the way in?"

"No, Lilian," he sighed, with a half smile. "He'll be a skeleton now and his teeth, because they're white, will just be very visible, even inside the black cave."

When we had all finished the ensuing conversation about the dental hygiene of pirates, we began a cautious exploration of the cave. I had a feeling, though, that we were not the first people to venture in there, as the treasure – being there as well as the long-dead pirate – must surely have attracted others to that place during the preceding hundred years.

We gingerly clambered – or fell – over obstructing rocks and each other as we passed beyond the entrance and entered the void. The deep and mysterious cave went in quite a way. Behind us, the view of the outside world diminished with every ungainly step that we took, quickly becoming just a small, angular hole of insufficient luminescence. Our eyes struggled to adapt to the smothering, impenetrable gloom that was now enveloping us. The sounds of our breathing became more pronounced in the still air. The dry walls deadened in an instant any groans or utterances that we made – we heard no echoes. Claustrophobia and fear sharpened our senses.

Each of us wanted to be the first person to glimpse that big, controversial pirate grin. I wondered whether we could recover the seafarer's sullied bones from the makeshift tomb and – if there was fine treasure to be found as well – who would get to keep what. I pondered the scenario for a moment and then put such unwelcome thoughts to one side.

Soon, we were advancing like a clumsy, nearly blind, desperate amorphous mass. For stability, we rested our hands on the cool walls. Our ten outstretched, inquisitive arms grasped voraciously as we ventured still deeper into the cold darkness.

Then Gly suddenly posed an interesting question: "Do you know if there are any bats in here, Idris?"

"*Bats?*" I asked, feverishly.

"Probably," Idris responded, in his usual cheery manner.

My heart started to race while I looked more attentively all around, although that was of little use in the virtual total blackness. I listened hard for the first signs of the coming to life of the little 'ratty vampires'.

"I think I'll go back out again now," I said as my fear of an encounter with the flying vermin began to reach a dangerously high level. Just then, I heard some movements from the end of the cave that we were walking towards.

At the same time, Alun shouted the desperate warning: "It's the pirate!"

A rush of wind passed my neck. Then someone grabbed me from behind and gave a blood-curdling groan of horror. In unison with everyone else, I screamed as loudly as I could and then joined in with the general frantic struggle to get back out to the safety of the daylight and the open beach. We ran into – and over – each other in our headlong dash to escape.

When we made it to the outside world, our panic kept

us racing along for about another fifty yards beyond the cave entrance. We finally collapsed shattered on the sand – shrieking, shaking and laughing with relief for a long time afterwards.

Unfortunately, we had discovered neither a pirate nor his treasure – only a cavernous home for the creatures of our vibrant and overactive imaginations, where so little seemed to have really existed – although *something* must have made that chilling noise at the back of the cave!

Our next port of call

After diverting into the picturesque and tranquil town of Saundersfoot for a break in one of its cafés, we continued our journey until we reached a stretch of barren, endless sand. We stopped there, to have our lunch and lay beneath the glorious sunshine with only the occasional sea bird for company. The faint wisps of cloud that bothered to turn up drifted lethargically as lofty gulls gently glided around in circles beneath them. We watched a quiet nature slowly pass by and, recuperated, eventually snoozed our way into the middle of the afternoon.

For the return journey, we were going to stroll along the tops of the cliffs for most of the way – thereby avoiding any possible further misadventures with the tides and barbed-wire-strewn beaches, and some other locations that we had detoured around earlier. They contained intimidating warning signs that read: "Mines – Keep Out!"

That only encouraged Alun to explain that any intruders were liable to be "blown to pieces!"

"Yes; they don't like trespassers much around here!" added Gly, flippantly.

Finally, we started to make our way home, to tell stories of cliffs and waterfalls and wobbly, pebbly things; to partake of a late dinner; and then retire to bed early. I was happy to be going back at last. I was getting quite tired now.

11

Fire and water

Go on Lilian! Jump off! It's only a few feet deep...

ONE MORNING, ROSA and I, in our improvised swimwear costumes, followed Alun, Gly and Idris out to the huge, grey Goscar Rock – the solitary, dominating projection that rose from the otherwise flat, golden, sandy shore that surrounded it. The Morgans assured us that it was a great place to play.

We waded through the knee-deep water until we could contain our excitement no more and ran the rest of the way, up to the front of the dark, impressive, twenty-foot-high elevation. I reached out and touched the rough, cold form, which was only now starting to be warmed by the morning's sun. The lower ten feet or so of it was generally darker than the rest and was covered in patches of thousands of tiny, light-grey barnacles, which were each about a quarter of an inch in diameter.

The Morgans immediately began their apparently effortless scaling of it. Its surface was not particularly damp or slippery – which made it relatively easy to gain a secure purchase, especially in those places that were covered in barnacles. I followed my more experienced companions and eventually, if slowly, managed to pull myself up towards the summit without encountering any great problems. Rosa soon joined me.

The view of the harbour had changed little from what I was used to. As I turned to begin earnestly playing games with the other children on the summit, I ignored all of the other worldly distractions, like the volume of dark water now commandingly splashing around the base – the creeping, autarchic presence that was so investing us.

Time had passed while I had been clambering around on the rock. The advance of the tide meant little when Alun invited me to jump into the sea, which he said was only a few feet down at that point. I hesitated and then did so, believing him. However, as I made contact with the water and started to go down, I suddenly realized that I was taking a long time getting to the bottom.

Daytime quickly turned to gloomy, green, aquatic twilight. The weighty embrace of a silent, ruthless, unforgiving sea was proving irresistible; I was being pulled ever deeper towards a frighteningly real, untimely, permanent rest.

"I must get out," I thought.

When I finally touched the bottom, I gave a huge push with my feet and stretched my arms upwards.

"Help! Help!" I called as I finally surfaced. I gasped and then involuntarily proceeded to swallow great mouthfuls of sea water. Gly swam over to me and I immediately and instinctively held onto her neck.

She cried, "Let go! You'll drown both of us!"

I held on in fear, though, so she pushed my head back and that made me swallow even more water. I tried not to panic. I reached out and desperately held onto her shoulders – following her directions – as she then proceeded to swim slowly towards the shore with me in tow. I staggered onto the beach, where I collapsed and lay for several minutes before I felt strong enough to return to the house.

Lessons

After I had arrived back from my near-fatal experience, Gly remarked that it would be a good idea if she gave me some swimming lessons. These were held in Mr Morgan's school, where there was a comforting familiarity with the surroundings – and a welcome absence of water!

About twenty chairs were set in line in the hall, one for each of us learners. We were instructed to stretch ourselves across them, following the instructions from Gly regarding the movement of our legs and arms.

I was unaware of one of the consequences of this until, one day, we were all taken to the harbour, where crowds of people were lined expectantly. I was told to take my turn and jump in as the other children had just done. We were there to show the crowds our capabilities as life-savers. I did as I was told and managed to perform well enough for the audience and my own wellbeing.

Only afterwards did I learn that the depth of the water – into which I had been told to throw myself for the sake of public entertainment and approval – was several times deeper than where I had earlier nearly drowned! However, I had been a good student at the swimming lessons and I did not need saving a second time – fortunately!

Theatre

The first time that the Morgans' children came home for the holidays, after I had arrived, we were all taken to see *La Bohème*. I remember little of the production itself, although I do recall that it involved a love story set in olden times – done to the accompaniment of quite a lot of singing – and one of the characters died in it.

Not frequenting such a style of entertainment – so different from what I was used to – I cannot pass an opinion of how original, good or bad it appeared in comparison with any other example of the art form. Nevertheless, it was my first experience of a proper adult theatre and the change was pleasant enough.

Going back home afterwards, we were party to another piece of theatre, this time on the streets. Several firemen were pushing along (or pulling, if in front) something that looked like a small, wheeled fire-fighting device.

There was no fire in the town as far as we could see and it was pointed out to me that Tenby already had an apparently perfectly adequate fire engine, so we had no idea why the firemen were bothering to run around desperately with another one. Nevertheless, they seemed to be doing it with a great sense of purpose, as though they were practising for some sort of an emergency where, unusually, the one fire engine would not be enough. It was not for our amusement then, presumably, that they feverishly ran up the road and around the corner like earnest Keystone Cops, although it was certainly strange to see.

Blackberry picking

One day, Mrs Morgan asked Alun, Rosa and me to collect some blackberries down one of the lanes where they grew. Mrs Morgan could then use them as filling in her home-made pies.

We got to where Mother Nature had been kind – where the bountiful shrubs grew – and immediately began pulling off all of the fruits that we could get our hands on. We put some in the basket and ravenously ate the rest.

When we had collected or consumed all that we could manage, we left the lane with a great sense of job satisfaction and full – if aching – stomachs, and lay down in a quiet corner of the adjacent field for a good, long, partly earned rest.

Scripts in the sky

As we all lay recuperating on the ground, staring up blankly at the sky, my attention was drawn to an apparition that caught the corner of my eye. I could not help noticing thin streaks of cloud that were beginning to make an appearance in the distance. Parallel, fluffy, white lines made their way from one end of the horizon towards the other and merged into the resident, sporadic cloud formations as they went. These were vapour trails of aircraft. I had seen similar sights before in ones and twos but this time I was quite surprised to see so many at once and together in such a neat pattern.

As they headed away and into the distance, I realised that another equally organised but smaller formation was meeting them from the other direction. For a reason that was not immediately apparent, I saw both groups start to go into a series of manoeuvres that destroyed all of their orderly arrangements.

The whole collection of trails began to scrawl new lines of curves and circles in the sky, leaving it scripted in monochromatic, ghostly messages. The legends of fleeting smoke trails suggested – or possibly belied, depending upon our understanding of them – the true explanation of what was happening.

Rosa and Alun were watching the unfolding events as well. As all three of us became quietly mesmerised by the impromptu aerial ballet, we pondered to ourselves its purpose and outcome.

Another ten minutes elapsed before the last of the aircraft appeared to fly away, trailing faint and dissipating vapour streams in the sky, some darker now than before – enigmatic attestations of recondite brethren that had so quietly come and passed our way.

The fruits of our labours

We returned home to a very appreciative Mrs Morgan, who made no comment about the excessive time that we had taken collecting her blackberries or of our mouths that were more mauve than usual through our recent vigorous consumption of hundreds of the delicacies. Our stomachs were still complaining a bit, though.

The next day, Mrs Morgan created her blackberry pies, made with very thin pastry around the outside, a thin pastry crust but filled with copious amounts of our berries. They were then cooked using the kitchen range.

Afterwards, she used the cream from the top of the milk for her portion, her husband's and Miss Dickinson's, while the rest of us just had the milk.

Unusual rain clouds
(Dramatization)

The following morning, I saw through my bedroom window what appeared to be a long, thick line of heavy, grey rain clouds moving slowly – all in the same direction – from horizon to horizon. I was puzzled because the rest of the sky was clear blue and we had had generally very good weather for the previous few weeks but now, in just one part of the sky, it looked as though torrential rain was about to be violently unleashed.

When I mentioned it to the others at breakfast, they said that they had noticed it as well and that it was not some heavy storm cloud but it was more like thick smoke. Mrs Morgan said that someone must have been burning something in the distance. When Idris said that he was thinking of cycling over to it, to have a closer look, his father adamantly told him to stay away, as it was dangerous and there could have been more fires breaking out near it.

Fallen eagle

While playing outside, later that morning, we started to hear some news about an aircraft that had crashed nearby. I was surprised about that, as I had heard no dramatic explosion nor seen any smoke rising from the approximate area of the crash site. We decided to investigate the rumours.

We walked for three or four miles until we saw some movement at the top of a hill in the distance. By the time we got to it, we saw about fifty other townspeople slowly circling around the broken remains of a large, green and grey twin-engined aeroplane. Although it still looked generally intact, it showed definite signs of damage that appeared to have contributed towards its ungraceful – and obviously unscheduled – return to mother earth.

Perforations – both large and small – were visible over the whole aircraft but were most prominent through the large, black crosses on the fuselage and wings, and on the large, black German swastika that was painted on the tail. The odd metal panel was bent up or missing, and the shiny glass nose looked a little worse for wear. The crew was fortunate, we were told; all of its members had survived, although not all were without injury.

Someone said that it had been on its way to attack the docks in the distance, when one of our aircraft had brought it down. Others said that the aircraft was on its way home only after having helped to start the terrible fire that had broken out there, and they pointed at the origins of the great column of smoke that I had seen since early morning.

A fearsome relative of someone based in the docks, said that she wished that she had reached the crashed plane and throttled the whole crew before the authorities had arrived, and was disappointed that the impact had not been more life-threatening for them. She kindly illustrated – with explicit hand gestures – how she would have dealt with any survivors.

We all stood before the German machine. Some of us stared with arms akimbo; others just slowly walked around the giant, lifeless, empty shell. We were confronting the once-terrible invader. Her back was broken. Her skin – to the touch of my curious, outstretched fingertips – was cold. Her corrupted, injurious, arrested heart had been taken from her. Prostrate before the spectators, powerless to intimidate, the lifeless giant bird – the fitting symbol of shattered Teutonic power – was going to soar no more.

The local attraction was soon to be taken away and, ironically, its metal used in the manufacture of more RAF aircraft! My nation's ability to defend itself seemed little

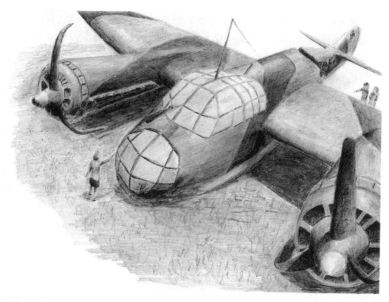

affected by the day's imperious events. Only in the distance
did anything seem awry.

Smoke
(Dramatization)

Nearby – perhaps a mile away and a couple of hundred yards
up in the air – the menacing horizontal column of thick, grey,
bubbling smoke was becoming more noticeable. Alun, who
had accompanied Rosa and me that morning, began making
his way towards it like a moth attracted to a light; Rosa and
I followed.

We eventually reached the centre of the smoke and stared
up at the immense – seemingly infinite – black form. It
was rolling around itself like a giant writhing 'serpent' in
guilt-ridden torment, which was twisting and contorting in
a vile dance of mesmeric anguish. It seemed held aloft as
though by the hand of something quite removed from the
everyday world. I feared it falling to earth, enveloping and
suffocating us long before we could ever outrun it. The dark,

demonic cloud dwarfed us, humbled us and left us helpless and entirely at its mercy. It was frightening and yet thrilling, in equal measure.

It was the ominous sinister messenger of a distant devastation. How distant was that devastation, I wondered. When I began to walk beneath the smoke – from one side of it to the other – I found that it took over a minute to do, such was its size. Its fiery origins were a place so far away that they could not be seen, yet only the intensity of an incredible inferno could have produced the unpredictable and awesome sight now above me. It blew across the landscape as though from the chimney serving the very fires of hell. The magnitude of the occasion became evermore shocking and profound, the more I comprehended it; I became transfixed.

The minutes passed: one... two... ten, perhaps. I suddenly thought of the angry woman by the crash site whose relative had been under the bombing at the docks. I came to understand her better when I thought of my mother, who had sent me to the country to be safe but who had remained in London. I thought of my sister, Nancy, who was with her. There were others, of course, with them in the city. I feared for them all.

There was far more to burn in the capital's docks than those distant ones now on fire; I surmised that its immolation would surely create a far greater spectacle than even the bold, black beacon of portent now present. I stood knowing that I could only hope that providence would be discriminating and protective, and – by its grace – I would still have a family to whom I would be able to return one day.

I left that place and returned to Tenby, with much to think about.

12

My secondary education begins

My fourth school in just over a year...
(Improvised dialogue)

HAVING LEFT MY nearby old junior school after attending for a few weeks, I now began my secondary education at the decades-old Tenby County School, an impressive large, white building at the end of a short, tree-lined path. I entered the playground specifically assigned to the girls and adjacent to the segregated one for the boys, conscious of being one of the new girls – the 'one from London'. My uniform, which had the welcome appearance of being new, consisted of a smart dark-blue gym-slip and a white blouse. Over my shoulder I carried a satchel, which contained my pencils and a lunchtime sandwich.

A couple of my old friends from my previous school were also due to start at this new one but I could not see them. I quickly realised that although I had passed the school's demanding entrance examination, they might not have and so would not be joining me.

I decided that I would have to try making some new friends. I wondered if I would be more successful in doing so if I seemed more Welsh and should try exaggerating the Welsh accent that I had already begun to acquire over the previous few weeks and combining it with some choice local phrases, but unfortunately I knew very little of the vernacular. There was the example that I had overheard only a few days earlier: I think that its correct pronunciation was 'Bachan diawl'. Unfortunately, it was an outburst and it meant something like 'bloody hell'. I feared that there were going to be limits as to how often it could be used in polite conversation and I knew that I had to refrain from using it too loudly in case a teacher overheard me – I did not wish to give the wrong impression about me. There was also the problem of manipulating conversations so that I could actually use the phrase and I was worried about what the other pupils would think of me if I responded to everything with 'Bachan diawl'!

"You're in Tudor," a girl suddenly uttered beside me. I turned and looked at her. She was quite like me, around the same age but a little taller.

"I'm in where?" I asked, confused by her statement.

"Your house. You're in Tudor house," she repeated. "Everything you do, you do in Tudor house... like me."

That did not help either. I wondered if a response concerning my place of residence would placate her. After all, that was a house. Then she began waving her uniform's tie at me in a slightly eccentric manner before explaining – as though it was the most important thing in the world – that my tie's specific colour meant that I was in the 'Tudor' group, one of three 'houses' within the school.

This, I suddenly realised, meant that I would probably be seeing a lot more of the girl than I would of some of the other children standing around me in the playground – those who belonged to different 'houses'. Despite her uncomfortably forward manner, I had the good sense to realise that it was probably wise to stay close to her for the time being. At least now, I thought, I had someone to converse with – even if what we were to speak about would not always make much sense!

The ringing of a hand-bell, which signified that we were to enter the building, suddenly interrupted my conversation with the girl. I presumed that the larger school bell, which was suspended high up in the building, could have been rung but that it was like all of the church bells in the country, which had been silenced for months. They were now only to be used to inform the population of an imminent invasion.

As only the hand-bell was being used on this occasion and there were no desperate warnings from the teacher like 'The Germans are coming! Run away, everyone! Run away!' it seemed safe to assume that there was no invasion taking place and that my new school life was to begin forthwith.

We all followed the teacher's instructions and entered the school en masse with an air of collective apprehension. (The teacher's instructions were only to go into the school – the fact that we did so with an 'air of collective apprehension' as well, was merely coincidental.)

At the front of the hall, which was not very large, stood the teachers, who were dressed demurely in their long, black gowns. They were mostly of the fairer sex and most of those had taken over the jobs of the male teachers who had volunteered to join (or had been conscripted into) the armed forces, to fight for king and country.

After a brief welcoming speech from the moustached headmaster – who did not look the happiest of souls – where he proclaimed without substantiation his belief that we were to be one of the best years' pupils ever in the history of the school, we had our morning prayer.

I was one of about fifty new children joining the school that day. After being allocated our respective teachers, we were dismissed from the assembly and left to follow them quickly through the draughty, labyrinthine corridors and up narrow, wooden, noisy staircases to our allotted classrooms.

As we sat down quietly behind our large, dark, wooden desks, my attention was drawn to the top of mine. I noticed that it had suffered the crazed scratching of apparently hundreds of poor souls who had been forced to sit behind it in previous years.

When I looked up again, I spied a coal fireplace nearby. It was not being used at the time because of the mild weather. I expected that I would be appreciating the heat of it in the colder months that would surely be arriving before too long. Near the blackboard, a gas light protruded from the wall. It conjured up unwelcome thoughts about how long the lessons in my new school could go on for, if the number of daylight hours would be insufficient.

"When I call out your name for registration, you will each respond clearly," the teacher abruptly instructed, capturing her young audience's attention.

We complied with due submissiveness.

"The timetable," she then started to explain and with that, I prepared myself for my first piece of written school-work: my compendium of subjects to learn and teachers whom I had to listen to and obey. Within the space of a few minutes, my intellectual journey for the coming year was to be mapped out.

"Mathematics and Arithmetic," she began and so, on my paper, it was written.

"English Language... English Literature," came next, signalling the beginning of my exposure to the works of the great novelists, playwrights and poets of recent and classic literature.

In time, the teachers and their chosen texts would inspire in me so strong a love of the English language that I would delight in spending long periods perusing the extensive vocabulary gracing the many imposing pages of my favourite heavy, leather-bound, comprehensive dictionary. When I first took hold of that tome, even the word 'vocabulary' was not part of my vocabulary. Eventually, though, many thousands of rich, complex and interesting words would become an indelible part of my spoken and written language.

"Drama," was next.

The same teacher taught both of the English subjects

and the Drama. It therefore seemed important to find her presence in particular – out of all of the teachers – agreeable, as my performance in so many subjects was dependent upon it. The time that I was to spend enthusiastically trying to perform well in her lessons, would not be wasted.

"Music," came next on her list.

The music department had a sparsity of instruments; however, everyone could sing (with varying degrees of success), so singing was to make up the essential part of the lessons.

The music teacher would forever listen for the occasional, stray, lilting Welsh accent, that gentle voice from the Valleys, a song from the heart. When he heard one, he would fête the individual, and then – when their confidence was up and their defences were down – he would charm or conscript them into one of the three house choirs. Particularly celebrated souls would become soloists. Thus, I would enjoy the distinction of the latter and embrace, with not a little apprehension, my duty to represent my house in the forthcoming inter-house competitions.

"Scripture Knowledge," appeared next on the timetable.

Being a Christian and having been involved with my old church in London, meant that I already had some understanding of this subject and – consequently – I was to enjoy it and do well in it.

"Latin," the teacher announced.

It initially seemed of little relevance; I was from London, where it had been heard infrequently to say the least. However, I was eventually to find it helpful when studying grammar and learning about the origins of other languages.

"French," she added next.

The woman teacher of the subject was of French origin. Her family and some of her friends were now far from her and living – and suffering – under Nazi jurisdiction.

At first I would find her strict but, in time, I was to grow to like her. She had a flat above the shops in the centre of town and, when I was later to progress with the language, she would offer to lend me some of her books on the subject.

When visiting her home, I would be amazed to find that she lived in such cramped conditions – unfortunate circumstances that she had never alluded to at school. They seemed wholly inappropriate for her status as an authority figure.

"Art," the teacher said next.

The subject was one in which I was to excel. In the class, I would soon draw a lovely Persian cat and proudly send the picture home to my mother, who would then lose it!

"History," came next in the syllabus.

I cannot claim that I was eventually to particularly master the subject.

"Geography," was next on the agenda.

I lacked both a good sense of direction and the ability to read maps. The foreign places studied were therefore to become merely where unusual things happened and located just not near where I was. Therein, my comprehension of geography ended.

"Science," next passed her lips.

Science, I felt, was something akin to geography, in that it seemed to be a subject more suited to boys than to girls. It was to command little of my attention.

"Domestic Science," came next on the timetable.

That ('cookery') seemed much more like a girl's subject. We girls were to be taught how to become dutiful housewives, caretakers of our future homes and connoisseurs of tasty, edible wartime rations. Our hungry husbands, returning in the evenings, could then look forward to casseroles of cabbages and carrots and similar treats, which I understood were just ideal after a hard, gruelling day of fighting down t' pit.

"PE," she added.

"PE!" I thought, enthusiastically. The subject seemed perfect for me, as I already had good all-round physical abilities. I was eventually to prove myself good at both hockey (which I especially enjoyed) and rounders. I also did athletics or – if the weather ever became inclement – I would go into the hall and do gymnastics.

When PE was to be undertaken indoors, my all-girl class was to have no need for modesty: we were to perform it in our navy-blue underwear. Frequently, I would be asked to demonstrate vaulting – and many other exercises at which I excelled – to the rest of the class.

I was to settle into my new school quite easily, perhaps because I could relate closely to the many female teachers, but probably because I was to behave well and try especially hard to succeed in my subjects.

The hand-bell rang, signalling the end of the registration period. My secondary education – my most important period of learning – had begun.

Homework and encouragement

Normally, after returning from a day at school, Rosa and I would not be allowed out. Instead, we sat around the kitchen table and did our homework, sometimes with encouragement from Mr Morgan. In the house, 'failure' had always been unacceptable for all of the Morgans and Miss Dickinson, and it was to remain so, even for their evacuees.

At other times – when we were at home and we had no school-work to do – we were made to take pride in our appearance; we cleaned our own tunics and pressed them.

The education that I was receiving was one of character building. It developed in me a resolve and a conscientious attitude that was to help me triumph over adversity at home and at school, and make me a better person.

Meanwhile, as the months rolled by, my classrooms filled with increasing numbers of evacuees – children like me who were leaving their families and their great cities behind them.

It was nice to have other children around me who were in a similar position to the one in which I now found myself. Unfortunately, with every arrival and with every story that they brought with them, of what was happening in their city, my fear – that I would never be returning home – only increased.

13

Letters, lessons and Nancy too!

Letters of a fragile future
I WROTE TO my mother about my new school and some of the exciting places that I had visited, and I am sure that I avoided mentioning the relatively dangerous areas that I still had a strong and fearless urge to explore. However, she must have read between the lines because a few days later she sent me a resplendent gold horseshoe charm for good luck.

One of her letters explained the circumstances of my evacuation to Wales more fully. After the fall of France, she urgently contacted our local Baptist church and sought its help in arranging my evacuation from London. The church promptly gave her the details of the Morgans – a household that was offering children like me the lifeline of a billet.

When she also began writing about Nancy's possible evacuation to Tenby, I wanted to make her think again, to warn her about my town's dangerous environment but then something made me think again and I hesitated. I read between the lines of *her* letters: Nancy could not remain in London much longer.

Miss Dickinson starts to give reading lessons
After I had been living in Tenby for a while, Miss Dickinson started giving private reading lessons to children from wealthy families, including, notably, the child of a distinguished captain.

Using methods that impressed her clients, which included various pictorial aids, she sat with her attentive pupil round a very large, oblong oak table in the drawing room. Near to them, a piano had been placed along one wall. On the opposite side was a large fireplace. At the side of this was a bell, which, if pulled, would be heard in the kitchen to summon the servants, if required.

After the lesson was finished, the child was collected by the parent or guardian and the fees for the one or two hours' services rendered were paid. At that point I would often be summoned, given a large, brown envelope – of which I was told to take great care – and instructed to deposit it at the bank. The payments for the lessons were enclosed.

Keeping a tight hold of my valuable package, I grimly executed my solemn duty with all haste and directly returned home, whereupon Miss Dickinson thanked me for my efforts.

Nancy arrives

Nancy eventually came to Tenby after my mother decided that it *was* the best place for her to live. She wasted no time relaying stories about some of the now unpleasant aspects of life back in London. German air raids, although becoming quite rare during the day, were increasing in frequency and intensity at night. As it was especially difficult to get to the outside shelter in the dark, Nancy and our mother eventually adopted the practice of going to bed in it even if there was no raid actually taking place. That way, if one did occur later, they would already be in the building and would not have to struggle to get to it.

Usually, the rising morning sun would drive back home any enemy bombers that were still around. Then the 'all-clear' siren would sound and Nancy and my mother could return to their more comfortable beds in the house. However, they generally found that it was not worth the inconvenience of getting up and going indoors – into cold beds – and would just complete their night's slumbers where they lay.

Although they were surrounded by the occasional falling bomb, it was not the fear of being hit by one that typically kept them awake but the sporadic blasts, throughout the night, of optimistic anti-aircraft fire from a gun position that was near to the house. Nancy said – with joyous and understandable relief – that she was looking forward to uninterrupted sleep from now on.

As we entered the house, Nancy expressed surprise at her impressive surroundings. In doing so, she reminded me of our good fortune – that we lived at that time in relatively safe and well-to-do surroundings.

As I read my mother's letter of advice and held her little money, both forwarded by Nancy, I again appreciated what we had in Tenby. Being told to value my life so much – being able to sleep so peacefully each night, with such confidence of awaking the next morning – only heightened my feeling of unease for those for whom I could do little but worry.

Christmas, more arrivals and the first eisteddfod
(Improvised dialogue)

At Christmas, Rosa's sisters Maggie and Gladys came to stay. The festive period was encumbered by necessary wartime thrift and rationing, and there was a great feeling of homesickness for us evacuees, but when the Morgans' children eventually returned from school, they sympathised with our situation and helped to make things much more pleasant.

By 1941, having been brought to an adequate state of readiness, I attended the school's inter-house singing competition – the eisteddfod. It was a celebration of Welsh culture that included other categories such as literature, art and the playing of instruments. It was held in the hall, which was prepared with seating for several specially invited personalities and other local people. The children who were not in any eisteddfod contest, had to squeeze into the remaining vacant area in front of the stage.

The event began with the battle of the choirs. Twenty or so boys and girls from each house sang their lungs out, trying to impress the judges and the opposition alike. After the songs of the throngs were completed, the competition of the soloist singers began.

"And now, Lilian Smith will sing..." was announced to the packed hall (the name of the song now escapes me, through the passage of time).

I automatically, if self-consciously and nervously, walked out onto the stage at the front as calmly as I could – as anyone could, whose heart was pounding as loudly and violently as mine was. I had already rehearsed a sort of apology speech, if my heart was ultimately to burst out from the fabric of my being and into one of the front rows of the audience: "Sorry!"

A sea of expectant faces lay before me; some, with their eyes staring and their mouths wide open, made me believe for a moment that they were getting ready to join in with my song. I quietly cleared my throat (and I had not actually started singing at that point), I took a deep breath and then began to perform – with dulcet, controlled tones – my long-prepared-for, emotional aria.

Minutes went by as I sang for the pride of my house and myself. I reached high notes and held them. I breathed hard for volume and endurance. The finale that I delivered was as though all of the discerning ears of a most musical nation were there as my judges.

When I finished and I was finally able to give my voice a rest, it was to respectable applause that I curtsied a little and confidently left the stage. (At least I hoped afterwards that it was for the song being well sung that I was receiving the accolade, and not just for the resting of my voice and my leaving the stage!)

Sheila Hurd sang next. Her presence on the stage commanded the attention of the audience. Her natural tones completely typified the voice of the local Welsh community. However, her overuse of facial expressions during her performance – to express sadness and pain – only gave her the appearance, somewhat, of someone for whom singing was not their first pleasure. Nevertheless, for what was after all a satisfactory rendering of pleasant intonations, I felt that the judges were almost certain to award the prize to her.

The third singer came and delivered another reasonable aria, although it was without quite as much success as the previous contender. After she had finished singing, she joined Sheila and me backstage, to await the deliberations and verdict of the judges.

After one of the invited guests had taken the opportunity to spend several minutes on the stage lecturing the school to a state of semi-consciousness with a prolonged speech about why he thought that the culture exhibited that day was so important within the realm of all of the other delightful expressions of culture that were so important, we soloist singers were brought back onto the stage and placed in a line, facing the audience.

The M.C. then praised the performances of 'the three singers who sang with gusto'.

"Who's Gusto?" the girl beside me asked, in a very quiet voice.

"Sh... One of the Marx brothers," replied Sheila, in an equally very quiet voice.

We three girls then gave each other sly glances and little smiles, and then left behind the slight dalliances with our sprightly imaginations and once more began concentrating on the unfolding dramatic proceedings before us.

The judges, who were to decide the winner of each category that day, solemnly passed a piece of paper – upon which was the name of the best singer – to the M.C. The M.C. looked at the piece of paper in his hand, then looked seriously at us for a moment and then shuffled up to the very edge of the stage, to face the hushed audience.

"The winner..." he slowly announced, "... of the eisteddfod soloist singing competition is... *Lilian Smith*, for *Tudor* house."

A huge grin came over my face and that of my singing teacher. I felt a great sense of achievement. My house cheered and clapped, and I was brought to the front of the stage. The children in the other houses did the decent thing and applauded as well, although they did so with understandably less enthusiasm than those in Tudor house (the teachers had previously instructed everyone to applaud, regardless of whom the winners were to be).

The winning houses in each event were awarded points and at the end of the day, the representative of the house with the most points was given a winner's prize. Whether or not my efforts contributed towards my house winning, I can now no longer say, but my performance in that eisteddfod was to be a source of pride and a valued memory that I would carry with me, always.

Miss Dickinson's den

Often in the evenings – and only when all of the homework was done – Miss Dickinson would invite us evacuees into her room for some story-telling. For that, we were arranged on the side of her bed, on the solitary seat or just wherever there was space for us on the floor. The seating arrangements were makeshift and definitely less than ideal, but we made the best of it.

Miss Dickinson chose stories that tended to suit the mood of us at the time, like *The Scarlet Pimpernel* or a ghost story. If it was read by the light of an atmospheric flickering candle, our senses were heightened and it made the stories more involving. It was generally impossible to complete a book in one session, so we frequently had to return to finish it another day.

As an interlude during the evening, Miss Dickinson would sometimes show us all sorts of strange African masks and other mementoes that she had gathered on her international travels as a missionary in Africa. The masks tended to be carved from wood and had real hair attached as well, which was usually styled in an absurd fashion. The finished articles were often quite grotesque in appearance and I was glad that I did not have any of them in my bedroom, spookily looking down at me at night when I was trying to sleep.

Sometimes, Miss Dickinson referred to many of those strange and stimulating objects when she was reading her stories – to help bring her tales 'more to life'. Later, after I had gone to bed, I found that the characters who had so effectively stepped out of the pages of her books often accompanied me on my journey to the land of Nod.

As my tired eyelids fell, fictional historical settings became real and solid to the touch. Celebrated personalities, villains and victims, accomplices and heroes – characters of a living literature all brought to life by candlelight stories

– led me away from reality for a few hours to their inspired magnificent world beyond the physical.

14

More summer adventures

Down t' pits
(Improvised dialogue)

DURING OUR NEXT summer holidays, the Morgans' children took us evacuees to some disused coal mines a few miles away to gather primroses that were to be sent to the Baptist Church in London.

Our journey took us through a gloomy, old, narrow railway tunnel that had rainwater trickling down its cool sides. We shouted when we were halfway through, hoping to hear some interesting echoes. We did so in vain though; it kept its silence.

As we started to enter a heavily wooded valley, I was surprised to see some uniformed men briskly laying barbed wire and digging around what appeared to be some sort of a concrete emplacement on the ridge above us. In the distance, I saw the silhouette of a similar pillbox-sized construction.

"What are they doing?" Alun asked his elders.

"Some sort of defence work," Idris replied, with some reservations. "Could be the Home Guard... or could be ordinary soldiers."

We looked towards the east – the direction the emplacements were facing – and then towards the west, at our town of Tenby and its surroundings, the last piece of land before the sea. For a few moments, we watched the soldiers toiling above the valley, to consider all that their work meant. Then Gly, reminding us of our mission, suddenly continued once more on the journey deeper into the wilderness. The fear of getting lost ensured that I vigilantly remained in the wake of my experienced guide. The rest of the party immediately followed me.

Tall, thick clumps of trees dwarfed and enveloped us. Some randomly threw their crooked, spindly branches around in the wind as though they were panicked by our presence and their freakish animation was meant to intimidate us and drive us away. The percussive arboreal commotion failed to either hurt or hinder us in our determined advance, and after about half an hour of meandering among the lofty, agitated life of the woods, we emerged into a 'clearing' – an overgrown landscape. It was an industrial graveyard. There were great arches; windowless, roofless buildings with unhindered views of the sky; and the skeletal remains of mine workings.

We made our way down to the patient ruins, which stood in silent melancholy awaiting our attendance. Scattered beside many of the crumbling and broken stone structures were heavy, corroding industrial relics – unwanted and discarded by a subterranean people at the end of their final day's toil.

Out of curiosity, I tried going into a nearby building. With no door, entry should have been easy; however, small obstructing plants – an incursion by nature – made the way difficult. Defiant, massive, grey and dirt-brown walls rose around me in proud silence as I eventually managed to get inside. Ivy, claiming the sides in her jealous grasp, added what little other colour there was to be seen.

The room was effectively empty. The useful machinery, presumably, had been scavenged; the fragments left behind had yet to rot or rust away. In the corner stood a cold furnace. On the floor were parts of the roof – dangerous, sharp-edged and unforgiving. Nearby, a wooden window with broken glass was ajar and giving pointless ventilation. Higher up,

another window was upside down; desperately, it was still hanging onto its one remaining hinge.

At my feet, green growths were entering the room from beneath – smothering the floor and reclaiming the dead space. The verticals of the disintegrating monument were succumbing to the life outside; penetrations were coming to fill the void within. It felt as though it was entombing me – it was a struggle to get out of the building and away from the stifling aura of decay. I was glad when I finally escaped. The ruin was a soulless place and had probably been so for a long time.

My companions and I left the site and took a small ten-minute walk to the actual mine area. It had fared no better through the years than the previous workings had – nature was busily reclaiming the land for herself and there were few of the mine's surface structures left visible. Gly led me to a place where bright yellow and mauve primroses lay all around and it was there that we spent much of our time picking the best of the flowers and putting them in our bags.

By the time I had collected quite a large number, I started

to wonder if we were actually taking too many; I was afraid that there would be none left to grow there anymore. Gly assured me that nature was a wonderful thing – that our taking of a few primroses, while leaving the rest of the place in peace, would do no long-term harm at all.

She pointed out how even the great monoliths around us, left behind by the miners, were now being slowly absorbed by the resurgent life around them. What was once grey was now becoming green; metal was turning to rust, and wood to dust. She said that the sending of those fragile plants – examples of a divine recovery after quite a traumatic upheaval – to a city troubled by war, would allow them to be used as tangible reminders that all hurt things will heal and become beautiful again in time.

Lady Evans's eggs

Nancy, Rosa's sister Gladys, and I regularly took eggs from Mrs Morgan's bantam chickens up to her wealthy friend, Miss Evans, who lived about a quarter of a mile away in a large detached house at the top of a steep hill. There was a long front garden that we had to walk up before we reached the entrance.

As we made our presence known, we were welcomed inside by a uniformed maid who invited us to sit in the oak-panelled foyer. She then disappeared with the eggs and other produce from Mrs Morgan into a long hall and closed the doors behind her. She returned a short time later to convey the thanks of Miss Evans, prefixing Evans with the title of 'Lady', which left us wondering whom she was talking about the first time that it happened, as we were unaware that Miss Evans was so titled.

When we left, we all felt a little privileged to have been entrusted with delivering such a scarce wartime commodity as a Lady's eggs and were relieved that we did not break any on the way.

Tea with the actress

Once, a famous actress, Sybil Thorndike, came to us for tea. The meeting between her and Mr and Mrs Morgan, was held in the drawing room. She had been invited to call after Mr Morgan had seen her in a recent production of Shakespeare's *Macbeth*.

The actress explained how she, her husband, and many other performers from the Old Vic theatre – where she had been working – were now touring Wales and putting on plays in different local communities as a kind of morale-raising gesture. They began doing their bit for the war effort in Wales after their London theatre had been damaged in an air raid, which had occurred a few weeks earlier.

Ms Thorndike was so different from Mrs Morgan, as she dressed more flamboyantly and wore lipstick. She had many amusing tales to tell her hosts. Some of these anecdotes were about the comical situations that arose now that she and all of the actors with her were being forced to improvise and make do with the minimum of production accessories, after so much material – such as their costumes – had been lost in the air raid.

15

Occupations

The shop

IN OUR HOUSE, there was a long, dimly lit passage. Halfway along it sat a huge trunk, which the Morgans' children used for transporting, by rail, their clothes and equipment for boarding school. One day, I accompanied Mrs Morgan to the end of the passage, where I stood before a heavy, blue, velvet curtain that was held by huge brass rings on a rod. I was invited to push that cloth aside, whereupon I was amazed to find that it covered the opening to the Morgans' family shop, which adjoined the house, and that I had just discovered their private entrance to it!

A glass counter stood in front of me, and to the right I observed wooden recesses that held skeins of wool in all colours and a variety of textures. Immediately parallel was another glass counter in which necklaces were meticulously displayed. A lot of these appeared to be white-faceted crystals interspersed with coloured stones. These apparently belonged to Mrs Morgan who was an expert on jewellery. She worked in a room next to the shop, repairing the expensive jewellery of the rich. This workplace of hers, unlike the shop front, was always untidy.

She sat in front of a wooden table, which was covered with brown cardboard boxes of all shapes and sizes. These held different types of beads that were used for her repairs. Right in front of the table she had several rulers, which were grooved, enabling her to lay the particular necklace in place for repair. For the more expensive ones, she knotted each stone individually. Large cardboard boxes, containing stock, filled one side of her room. To the right of it were several rails of clothing.

Her other interest was needlework, in particular smocking. She made dresses in pastel shades of crêpe material and used coloured smocking across the chest. She also made scalloped hems, which she painstakingly stitched with silk thread, for the garments destined for her youngest child, Ray.

To the left of the shop was a display counter. This held a lot of leather items such as purses and gloves. Miss Dickinson made most of these as I discovered when going to evening classes, which she held in a room in the local Congregational Church one night a week. Her classes were always well attended, often by women wishing to sidestep the austerity of rationing by learning to make their own luxury items. Miss Dickinson's expertise also included the making and selling of exquisitely embroidered cushion covers and tablecloths.

I occasionally served in the shop after I had been in their household some time. I found it exhilarating, especially when making a sale. If it was difficult in any way or the customer wanted jewellery – a commodity that Mrs Morgan liked to sell personally – I rang a hand-bell. Mrs Morgan would then come to the front of the shop and take over the sale.

The joy of music
As time went on, Miss Dickinson played a more prominent role in the household. We heard her frequently rowing with Mr Morgan. Christian names were emphasized so loudly that Mrs Morgan had to intervene. She had to appease both parties, having loyalties to both.

Mr Morgan spent less and less time in the house; he

went either to his school or to his allotment, where he grew potatoes and fruit. On visiting him at school, I found him beside the fire in his study. The radio was blaring. He was looking positively happy, in contrast to his usual serious side in the house. He must have found the freedom to listen to the radio as he wished somewhat liberating – the Quaker environment at home prevented it being listened to at any time, except at Christmas.

He frequently had rehearsals for one thing or another and I often found him with a music teacher in attendance. She was short and had straight, dark hair. She wore glasses and had a large nose and protruding teeth. Her placid personality overrode her 'defects'. She had an auburn-haired daughter and lived a few streets away from the school. I once went with Mr Morgan to her house, to rehearse a song.

The narrow street door of the white-clad exterior opened to reveal the smallest room in which I had ever seen anyone trying to live. The place was spotlessly clean though. Immediately opposite the door stood a brown, burred-effect piano. Small ornaments were visible and sprigs of flowers completed the pleasantly quaint scene before me.

She welcomed us with a huge, beaming smile. Her happy disposition helped all of us overcome the discomfort of the small room, which suddenly became even more cramped when she added the extra chairs for us.

After a short while of practising the song, the door unexpectedly swung open to reveal her daughter. At this point, Mr Morgan made his excuses and left. He decided that further practises would take place at his school instead (where he could at least be assured of more room!).

A new sister to return to...
In 1941, my mother wrote to inform me of the arrival of Joan – my new sister! The name of Joan's father was not mentioned.

Sundays

Sundays were spent going to church. Prior to this, Mr and Mrs Morgan were given their breakfast on a tray in their bedroom. Sometimes I gave it to them if the maid was busy.

At first, I attended on Sunday afternoons. Later, they took me along in the mornings as well. The church was situated at the end of the tree-lined road where we lived, so the walk at least was enjoyable. As we entered, Mrs Morgan took her place among the choir at the front of the church.

The services were long and boring. I noticed that the preacher, a grey-haired man with a healthy complexion, always talked to Mr Morgan afterwards. I realised that the Morgans had a close attachment to the church and its preacher, and their friendship with him was such that he always spent Christmas with us.

The next eisteddfod

Although I had taken extra singing lessons with Mr Morgan, Sheila Hurd – who was my greatest rival – had also improved markedly by the time of the next eisteddfod.

During the competition at school, when I went out onto the stage for my solo performance believing that I had a good chance of defeating the opposition, it was me who was beaten by Miss Hurd, because of her much-enhanced voice.

I was very disappointed, especially after all of the efforts that others and I had gone through to ensure that I would win. It was the catalyst that caused Miss Dickinson to start taking a special interest in my singing.

Singing lessons from the 'master'

When I became a teenager, I began to be more aware of situations involving the Morgan family and took more notice of their relationships. Miss Dickinson, for instance, particularly liked Mr Owen, the organist at the church. She would go out of her way to speak to him in flattering tones after the service.

He was a few years younger than she was. He had fair, wavy hair, a ruddy complexion and steely blue eyes. He always looked bemused when she approached him. The common bond between them was music. Besides playing the organ, he gave lessons in singing for which he was well paid. Many pupils went to London and into operas after being taught by him.

"Could you give Lilian a few singing lessons?" she asked him one Sunday.

He replied in the affirmative and so it was that, one day, I accompanied Miss Dickinson to his house. It was a few streets away, adjacent to the sea front.

"Come in!" was the welcoming bid as the door we were about to knock on, was opened. The room that we entered was unlike any other I had seen. A large grand piano was immediately visible. There was also an Indian carpet – a multicoloured tapestry with a light background – lying on the floor. Silver candlesticks and large vases with other expensive items gave an air of opulence. All that I saw was most unexpected, as Mr Owen always dressed in a mundane fashion. There were large bay windows draped in fancy net curtains and heavy, beige velvet curtains either side, with tasselled ties.

He indicated a velvet-upholstered armchair for Miss Dickinson to sit on. I stood next to him as he sat down on the stool at the piano. He then took a long time testing my vocal abilities. Most of the time was spent teaching me how to reach high notes and alter the shape of my mouth when doing this.

Miss Dickinson disappeared into another room to talk to Mr Owen at the end of the session. Mr Owen emerged after a short time and said he was impressed with my voice to the extent that he would give his time teaching me for free, adding enthusiastically that I could become a great singer!

Miss Dickinson and I went many times to his house and, as I did so, I gained confidence.

My Tudor house at school eventually decided to keep me as their soloist singer and it was left up to me to prove, at the next eisteddfod, that Miss Dickinson's and Mr Owen's faith in my abilities had not been misplaced, and that their philanthropic endeavours had not been wasted.

16

More summer holidays

Nancy almost drowns!

MY NEXT SUMMER holidays started with Nancy and me going to the beach. After several minutes in the sea, I decided to relax and sunbathe on the sand while Nancy remained splashing around in the water.

Suddenly, I heard my sister in the distance calling out for help. I sat up and, after scanning the waves for a few seconds, I saw her desperately flapping her arms about as she struggled to stay afloat in water that was obviously too deep for her small size. I looked around but, in the commotion being made by all of the other playing and screaming children, no one appeared to be taking any notice of Nancy's plight. I quickly got up and began wading into the sea.

As I made my way out and the water got deeper, I had to

swim the rest of the way. When I reached Nancy, I managed to take hold of her using the life-saving skills that I had learned only a couple of years earlier and which were now being tested for real. I began pulling her back to safety – back to shallower waters, where I was able to wade the last few yards.

Nancy and I struggled to the beach, where we collapsed. A small, curious crowd belatedly started paying attention to the drama that had been unfolding only a few yards from them. Nancy was coughing and spluttering a lot but did not otherwise appear to be too seriously harmed; I think that she had drunk most of the seawater that had entered her mouth, instead of breathing it in. Perhaps that helped to stop her drowning but it would probably have been better if she had simply spat the stuff out. Then again, as I had recently experienced when I had almost drowned, one does not always behave completely rationally when the prospect of death looms large and panic begins to set in.

After Nancy had rested for a while, I decided to take her back home. I felt very pleased with myself, that my deed had resulted in nothing less than my sister's life being saved.

The next great expedition
(Dramatization)

Our next great journey with the young Morgans took us first to an old, small, ruined farmhouse. I went inside the building and viewed again the landscape outside, of tall weeds and tangled green grass, and imagined a beautiful picture of the past but my mind's eye could not ignore the room in which we stood, of determined decay, of cobwebs and spiders, and skeletons of rats now exposed through time's ravaging of the dying wooden structure. We left the place to its wanton interminable decline.

Arriving at an old church, Rosa bravely tried some of the water from its holy well and said afterwards – rather unsurprisingly – that it tasted like 'water' and that it had made her 'less thirsty'. Nevertheless, at no time was I tempted to copy her.

When some brown and white cattle appeared not too far away, Idris – through an inspired sense of humour, poor eyesight or both – cried out: "The bulls are coming!"

As though in fear for her life, Rosa immediately put her hands up to her cheeks and started screaming. Then, feigning virtual hysteria, she threw her arms in the air (not literally, of course)... *"Weee... Farewell two arms!"*

She waved them around a lot and began running away, indirectly towards the other end of the field. We all joined her, moving faster in the opposite direction – away from the 'killer bovines' – to exit the field at a point that we had not initially envisaged.

When we had made it out of the field and looked back from behind the safety of a good strong wooden fence, we noticed that our commotion in running away had so startled the beasts that they had actually started running away from us! The fearsome- (or frightened-, depending upon one's eyesight) looking creatures had now congregated at the other end of the field.

After a more careful inspection of the 'bulls', we pointed out to Idris that they were surprisingly bereft of horns – suggesting strongly that they were in fact... cows!

His response was that that just showed us how cunning the 'bulls' were – that they would so craftily remove their horns in order to look like cows. Remembering that we were always meant to be on the lookout for anything suspicious – such as German spies dressed as nuns – and having just discovered several very suspicious 'bulls' that were 'disguising' themselves as cows, he suddenly had a flash of heightened inspiration.

"They could be spies!" he announced. "And we should be proud of ourselves for having found them out."

I responded with, "Who's ever heard of 'bull-spies'?"

"Bulls can't make pies," Rosa quickly and quite rightly pointed out. She then spent a moment showing us how difficult it would be for them to do so without the dexterity that hands afford.

"Nature can be so cruel sometimes," said Gly, sympathising with their 'plight'. "But bulls do make the perfect spies because no one would ever expect that spies would come in the guise of cows."

"You don't refer to cows as 'guys'," said Idris, correcting her.

We eventually parted from them but not before we gave them a warning, that if they did not stop their 'spying' forthwith then we were going to tell Winston Churchill about them... *"Boo – you spies! Go back to Germany, where you came from!"*

Alun added, in a moment of patriotic zeal, that he was sorely tempted to put them up against a wall and shoot them as the 'spies' that they were, and was only not doing that because he lacked a rifle... and a wall.

After travelling along some country lanes, many of which

were 'sunken' (meaning they were about three or four feet below the level of the surrounding fields), we came to a couple of castles in quite quick succession. The first was formidable-looking and in fine condition but the second, which we climbed all over, was a ruin. (It was a ruin before we climbed all over it!) Leaving the castles behind, we next made our way to some little inlets of water – a revolting haven of mud-flats for a multitude of bird species. Strange-looking waterfowl – birds with long, pointed beaks – inquisitively and repeatedly probed beneath the surface of the unpleasant dark-brown 'ooze' in search of their meals.

"Ugh!" was the consensus from us evacuees as we viewed with perplexity the enthusiasm with which the hungry little foragers strove to find their next piece of filthy subsurface food.

Unlike their human counterparts, the bird's food was not rationed. They could contentedly eat as much of it as they could find. Only when the tide was to return and cover the area again later that day, would they have to stop their gorging. In that sense they had the advantage over us, but – ugh!

When Gly said that the next field appeared to be full of marsh mallows, our group of excited young girls ran to behold the sight of so many candies. We were to be sorely disappointed though. The 'marshmallows' that we imagined we would find, turned out to be only hundreds of pink 'marsh mallow' plants.

Gly explained that the roots of those plants could be used to make the sweets. However, when she admitted that there was no way that any could be made that afternoon, she gave up trying to make things any better for us. She left it, instead, to the weather to continue making things worse – rain appeared to be in the offing. Fearing that we would be caught in it, we decided that we would not look at any more sights but begin making our way back without delay.

We walked with an increasing pace and almost made it home exhausted yet dry, when the rain that had been at hand for so long became the torrent on our heads, and we made it home exhausted and soaked instead!

17

Another year

Why talking in bed was not a good idea
DURING MY EARLY period in Tenby, Miss Dickinson would frequently question my manner of speech and threaten, if it was not to her liking, that she would wash out my mouth with soap. The other evacuees were equally imperilled by what they cared to utter. We were also told that talking in the bedroom at night was forbidden.

After a short time, I foolishly ignored the golden no-speaking rule and, although I should have expected it, I was still amazed when I was confronted by Miss Dickinson's angry figure of immediate retribution standing ominously in the bedroom doorway. Given her stance, I felt very apprehensive about what was about to happen to me.

"Get out of bed!" she yelled. "Get a broom and sweep the garden and clean out the chicken shed!"

Her face was flushed with anger. I looked askance at the instruction, as I knew that they had an allotment where they grew potatoes and fruit, but the only 'garden' was a back yard with a small patch of flowers near the door and a long path down the middle. To the left was a high bank of worn grass and mess from the chickens. To the right was a chicken shed, which had long wooden perches, straw nests and filth everywhere. Next to this was a long shed of which part was given to the younger son to use for various chemical experiments.

"I've got my nightdress on," I protested.

"You will do as I say!" was the curt reply.

One of the girls in the bedroom handed me their coat to put on over it. Unfortunately, it was small and the sleeves were too short. It was in this inadequate outfit at dusk that I made my sorry way to the garden, to view with dismay the task before me. I knew that the quicker I worked, the sooner I could go back to bed. I learned my lesson well; the inventive, unpleasant consequences of a few words foolishly spoken out of place made me resolved not to make the same mistake in the future.

Taking the washing

One day, I was asked to go with Rosa to visit a woman in one of the back streets. The reason was to take Mrs Morgan's washing there. We found the narrow street of small houses in which the woman lived. I went up to her house and knocked on the door. The lady who opened it was both fat and old.

"Thank you, Lily," she replied when we gave her the large bundle. "I'll have the washing and ironing done by..."

She stated the day and when we returned as arranged, we were handed the immaculately ironed articles. As I took hold of them, I noticed her red, rough-looking hands resulting from the endeavour. We gave her the small payment for this in an envelope and left.

The new headmaster and Lady Macbeth

When I was thirteen, the school that I attended suddenly had a new headmaster – Mr Gibson. He had dark hair, a rather round face and glasses to match. Like me, he originally came from a long way away. I felt that I could particularly relate to him, as we were both, somewhat, 'outsiders'.

He taught art – a subject in which I excelled. He frequently put my work on show, to inspire the other pupils in my class. I became his trusted pupil and I was often sent to fetch articles to the classroom from his all-important roll-top desk in his study.

He was quite a disciplinarian – instructing us to neither slouch nor indolently rest our elbows on our desks. Instead, we were always to sit alert and upright behind them. Although he was as strict as the previous headmaster had been, I nevertheless found him a pleasant gentleman.

In time, I began excelling at English. My increasing abilities frequently earned me parts in plays that were read aloud in class; one part in particular was Lady Macbeth, a character from the same Shakespearean play in which Sybil Thorndike had recently acted.

Ms Thorndike's visit to the Morgans' home might have inspired me to give my diction a more confident and professional sparkle. My class certainly seemed to enjoy my subsequent melodramatic performance as much as I did.

Ada

Ada, one of the maids, laboured to serve the household's living requirements and maintain the premises' virtually impeccable appearance but she often found her work criticised by Mrs Morgan. For instance, she frequently spent ages cleaning the utensils in the kitchen, only to see them all thrown back into the sink – to be washed by her all over again – when Mrs Morgan considered the results were not good enough!

Ada rued being in the employ of such a hard-to-please person and desperately wanted to work elsewhere. For that, though, she needed a good reference; whether she could have expected a good one from the Morgans, was a moot point.

Ada had no family to whom she could return. She constantly worried in case the Morgans were to sack her and make her homeless, for she was only entitled to her accommodation as long as she was employed in the house. If she had just walked out of the job and the house, she would have made herself homeless.

The poor young woman felt that she had virtually no choice at all – except to remain the lowly unfortunate, endure the hard work and criticisms, and then retire to her private place of solace – her bedroom – at the end of each working day. She spent many a tearful time there, alone in her own personal space, bemoaning her predicament.

The next eisteddfod

A more pleasant distraction for me was my next eisteddfod competition, in which Sheila Hurd sang against me once more.

For my performance, I took a deep breath and then began singing of the Welsh hills and a land of my brothers. I was assuming a certain artistic licence, as I did not come from the former and I was several brothers out when it came to the latter (I only had Arthur – and he was certainly not Welsh). Fortunately, I was not being judged on the geographical or numerical accuracy of what I was singing about.

I received a considerable ovation from the audience and personal congratulations from the M.C., and by the time of the awards – despite my reservations – I was brought once more to the front of the stage to reclaim the title of best soloist.

The time that I had spent training in the extra singing lessons had been vindicated. The challenge had been risen to; the faith that my benefactors had had in me, gladly repaid.

18

The bicycle journeys

To the docks
(Dramatization)

WE EVACUEES USED to go cycling sometimes. On one occasion, on hired rickety bicycles, Alun led Rosa and me on a long ride into the countryside. The roads were generally quiet, as petrol rationing had immobilised much of the motorised transport.

We passed secluded grey-stone cottages and the odd hamlet before stopping to investigate a large, decrepit, mediaeval-looking building, which was surrounded by several undulating grassy mounds – presumably some related structures that had become buried over time.

The roof and most of the floors were gone, and the rooms looked more like greenhouses minus the glass, such was the quantity of plants that were incongruously living there. A large, grey-stone fireplace tempted us to climb up it but we sensibly resisted the urge, fearing that we would get ourselves very dirty and possibly even stuck! The labyrinthine ruins encouraged us to play hide and seek for a while, after which we returned to our bicycles for some refreshments. As we sat eating and drinking, Alun informed us that we would eventually be seeing another castle.

Another castle, I thought. Once upon a time, when I played with my doll, I stuck her at the top of her 'castle'. She was the archetypal damsel in distress, to be rescued romantically by her gallant knight in shining armour. At that time, I relished the idea of being just like her – atop my own castle – but now that I had the very real opportunity to live out my childhood fantasy, I declined. It was not so much that my older years had curbed my childish enthusiasm; it was just because real life now proved to be so very different from what I had been expecting when I was younger.

Firstly, the only way that I could now become trapped at the top of my castle would be if I ascended the nearby tall and dirty chimney and then deliberately jammed myself at the top of it. However, I felt that that would somewhat destroy the magic of the whole experience.

Secondly, historically – as far as I was aware – no knights in shining armour ever rescued sooty damsels who were stuck up smoke-stacks.

And lastly, the chivalrous days of heroic knights seemed long gone. For the first two reasons, I never 'trapped' the heroine of my youth – my doll – at the top of her castle by ramming her up a chimney and, for all three reasons, I was not about to do it to myself.

I feared that any climb up a chimney now would not be a sooty prelude to the wonderful courtly romance of my dreams: only the beginning of a protracted period of altitude-related misery. My companions were the kind of children who certainly could have rescued me but I doubted the enthusiasm with which they would have done it.

I expected that Alun, for instance, would have eventually gone for help but only after detouring first to look at some more castles for a few hours. Rosa, meanwhile, being the friend that she was, would probably have chatted to me – to keep up my spirits – but if anyone had passed by, she would not have been too shy to make a bit of money out of the occasion…

"Roll up. Roll up, ladies and gentlemen. Come and see the silly girl stuck at the top of the chimney. Only threepence a gawp."

"Oh, hello. And who are you?"

"Lilian, ma'am."

"Pardon?"

"Lilian!"

"Lilian... Oh, I see. And are you often getting stuck up chimneys, then?"

"First time, actually... I'm hoping a good knight'll come along soon and rescue me."

"You're hoping for a what?"

"A good knight!"

"Oh, good night, then."

And then they would have just left me there! What a cheek! However, if I had become stuck as soon as I had entered the chimney, Rosa would just as likely have offered my dangling legs – swinging helplessly at the bottom – to passers-by as a different form of entertainment...

"Welcome sir... madam. Would you each like to take hold of a leg and make a wish? Only sixpence."

Sixpence. **SIXPENCE!** Threepence a leg! Well, Rosa, what kind of friend are you, I would have wondered. Things could have been even worse though. If I had been stuck up the chimney at the same moment that a surprise German landing was taking place, Rosa could have been forced to use me as a weird human-bell hybrid in order to raise the alarm for the local populace. Pulling alternately on each of my legs, she would have given me fervid instructions to go 'Ding' and 'Dong' in the most campanological of ways, in time with each of her desperate tugs...

"Quick, Lilian! The Germans are coming! It's the invasion! As I pull, sound the warning."

"Ow! Oh, must I? OK, then. Here goes. Ow! Ding-dong! Ding-dong! Ding-dong!"

"Lily..."

'Ding-dong indeed! What a liberty!' I would have thought to myself.

"LILY!" snapped Alun, bringing me back from my imaginary campanological chimney ordeal. "Wake up. We're going now, all right?"

The town
(Dramatization)

After leaving the great 'castle' with its 'chimney of woe', we eventually freewheeled down a steep hill into a quaint little town. Unfortunately – and for what felt like the hundredth time that day – we had to struggle to peddle up the next hill.

Along narrow, winding streets, we unexpectedly passed a few wrecks of houses – modern-day ruins for a change and presumably the result of German bombing.

"I wonder if they all got out," Rosa mused, of the buildings' erstwhile tenants.

No sights or sounds of destruction had visited us in Tenby apart from the one aircraft that crashed nearby. However, people not so far away were fighting a war – were having real life-or-death struggles. We were stilled before our grim reminder.

We continued with our journey and soon came across the town's castle that Alun had told us about earlier. Recently built terraced houses were incongruously standing beside the huge, grey fortress – a fine example of intact mediaeval military craftsmanship, which dominated the town that had literally grown attached to it. The amalgamation of different building styles presented a strange sight. The nobler presence, with its massive round towers, numerous arrow slits and high defensive battlements – the substance of its being was the very embodiment of belligerence – proudly and stoically stood now as the indefatigable indigenous fighting spirit. The humbler dwelling next door – the beginning of the High Street – had two small flower-pots on its window-sill outside.

Upon the castle's battlements, British soldiers – modern-day 'knights' – were manning several mighty anti-aircraft guns. Awaiting the next deadly aerial armada, their weapons were silhouetted and elevated defiantly high up into the sky.

The docks
(Dramatization)

After passing scenes of increasing urban destruction, followed by an impressively large grey fort, we eventually came to the beginning of a vast harbour. Beside various jetties that had large numbers painted on them, ships of even the largest size were being easily accommodated as they completed, from oversees, their latest delivery of desperately needed food for this nation's larder, and material for its armed forces.

There were two small forts nearby with large guns projecting from them. Across the water, large construction sites were being created, as though the area was to become even more significant as a vital lifeline for the country in the near future.

Alun drew our attention to some buoys floating on the water, and then casually began walking away.

"Oh, *those* buoys," said Rosa, feeling a bit foolish after a momentary misunderstanding. "I thought you meant..."

I held my silence.

Around the docks were several large, grey supply ships that had probably just come from the United States of America. The Atlantic Ocean, which they would have sailed across, was deemed a vast hunting ground by the Germans, who ruthlessly employed numerous weapons of war there – most notably deadly U-boats – to stalk their daring, vulnerable prey. The merchant crews of those cumbersome and defenceless transports must have been particularly brave to attempt the dangerous journey and would surely have been very grateful for the protection afforded to them by any accompanying escort warships – two small examples of which were docked nearby.

Now, the transports were at rest. They lay along the dockside, where many tall cranes were busily (or nosily, perhaps) dropping their inquisitive chains (each of which had a hook at the end) into the innards of the ships, probing them and removing the heavy, precious cargoes contained within. Other cranes alongside, which were now satisfied, stood smartly to attention, patiently awaiting their next important consignment.

The dock did not seem to be the preserve only of the Royal Navy and its merchant cousin; many other small craft were to be seen on the wide expanse of water, including a few fishing trawlers. They must have been quite daring to sail out to sea, to help replenish the nation's desperately needed food stocks. A German U-boat or bomber could probably have easily sunk one of those little ships (or, more accurately, big boats).

Beyond a promontory, a dozen large, silhouetted aircraft rocked ever so gently on the sparkling, rippling water. They had the slightly surreal appearance of being on a completely waterlogged airfield but these were flying boats, their domain was the water, and they used their hulls and floats for buoyancy upon it.

One aircraft on a large trolley had been pulled up onto a ramp. A couple of mechanics, balancing on the wings, were working on one of its four huge engines. The men were about twenty feet up in the air and they sometimes had to lean over the edge of a wing – becoming virtually upside down! – in order to reach a difficult part of the engine.

While Alun continued to scrutinize the proceedings, Rosa began wandering away and then returned a minute later with a cheeky half-smile on her face.

"You know what, Alun?" she asked rhetorically.

"What?"

"You're looking at their aeroplanes."

"Er, yes," he said, after a pause.

"Well… they might think you're a spy."

"What?!" replied Alun, taken aback by Rosa's sudden alarming announcement.

"That's what spies do. *They* look at aeroplanes." Rosa thought for a moment and then continued, "You could get put up against a wall and shot!"

"*And* they've got the walls to do it with," I added cheerfully.

Alun looked at us momentarily with an expression of paternal disappointment, shook his head and then carried on with his fearless and 'daring' plane spotting. We were about to return to the town, when Alun's aircraft-sensitive ears pricked up at the sound of a distant aeroplane. It appeared smaller than most of the other flying boats (it really was smaller – it did not just look like that because it was far away!).

Like a fastidious, magnificent swan, it gently circled and then began easing back its two engines. Its considered graceful glide down to the water ended with dramatic splashes accompanied by our calls of "Oh, oh!" and spontaneous applause for the unexpected majestic aerial display. It landed not far from the other planes and almost came to a rest before revving its engines once more, to make the short journey to be with them again.

Almost immediately, one of the larger aircraft that had remained motionless as the smaller one was landing suddenly spluttered into life. One after the other, its four powerful engines – the same types as the ones that we saw being worked on earlier by the 'occasionally upside down' mechanics – revved loudly and then calmed down a little as, ever so gently, the great flying boat began its forward momentum.

Like a sprinter awaiting the starter's gun, it lined itself up with the straight part of the channel, which ran the length of the harbour, and then paused. We all looked in that other

direction – the way it was facing – and, seeing no obstacles before it, began giving encouragements to the huge 'reluctant beast'.

"Come on! You can do it!" we urged the hesitant, tired, war-weary old bird. We shouted for a minute or so and that seemed to do the trick. The plane turned a little and looked at our gesticulations through its cockpit eyes. As though it was receiving a new spirit of determination from our calls of support, the battered beast lined itself up once more, to face the long line of the channel.

The humming, idling engines suddenly roared furiously back to life. With this power, the grey mass soon began to make a considerable speed along the water and, in doing so, created a turbulent wash that rose up and caught the vortices of air that were pushed back by the vast, spinning propellers. The ensuing fine spray – carried on the wind – lightly sprinkled itself onto our faces like droplets of a cool, nervous sweat as the lumbering plane precariously passed us by.

"It's not going to make it!" said Alun, alarmed at the rapidly diminishing amount of water that was left ahead of the aircraft. "Go on! Give it more power!" he desperately urged.

Rosa and I got so engrossed in the developing situation that we too began imploring the faltering plane to take off instantly. We could not take our eyes away from the spectacle that was fast approaching – the aeroplane's imminent tragic collision with the land mass in the distance!

We distinctly – and almost incredibly – heard the pitch of the engines increase as they strained even more, so that, in the whole of the docks, nothing sounded greater than the noise of our too-heavy machine, desperately struggling against its own weight to get airborne. Like a high-speed racing boat, it threw up copious amounts of spray behind it. Recklessly, though, it continued heading straight for the land mass in front with an urgency that seemed almost suicidal.

As it began to run out of water, it perceptively began to move towards one side of the channel – apparently a drastic attempt to exploit the river's natural curve in order to gain a few extra seconds of time in which to take off.

Suddenly, there was a small gap in the spray, and then another. We held our breath. Our plane, fighting the river, was pulling away from it, even if only for a few seconds but those few seconds were not to be enough.

It returned to the water and bounced, throwing up another enormous spray. It was now approaching the land ahead too fast: it would be unable to stop or turn away before it would crash into it. But suddenly, it appeared to have one chance left: to take off once more: to get airborne and stay up. Fail – and it would never have the height to try again.

With one final effort, the engines screamed and the propellers thrashed wildly in their determined attempts to haul their heavy aircraft up one last time. A simple take-off had now become a matter of life and death. From beyond the point of no return, the aircraft strove to release itself from the water's tenacious grip.

It got up... definitely... just. The vital seconds passed – two, three, four, five. It was staying up. It was still in the air and getting higher with every second that passed but getting far too close to the hills in front. With moments to spare, it desperately banked sharply to the left, clearing the land mass ahead of it by the smallest of margins. As it now headed straight for another hill, its screaming engines pulled it to the right this time, searching for a gap. It found a space ahead of it and climbed and fought to reach it. Higher and then higher still it flew until, finally, the salvation of the open sea and an unobscured sky lay before it. It had made it.

Easing itself upright and with the need for a maximum exertion now passed, the engines calmed down and our aircraft settled into a gentler ascent into the sky. Its crew's time – to meet their Maker – was not up... not *yet* at least. With beguiling grace, the grand, grey machine headed out, alone, across the waiting sea.

I now turned my attention to the small crowd that we had attracted – the tiny group of people who had bothered watching, with us, the life-or-death struggle out on the water. It saddened me that only about half a dozen people, including a couple of uniformed men standing beside us, had shown any interest in such an earnest struggle for life. It was as though it was a usual, everyday occurrence for the people of the area that an aircraft in the harbour almost crashed. I thought that it should have warranted far more attention from them. One of the 'soldiers' (I was assuming that the uniformed men were soldiers), in a foreign accent, asked us if this had been our first time visiting the docks.

"Yes," Rosa and I replied, although Alun said that he had been there a couple of times before.

By this stage of the war, it was not unusual to see military personnel walking around and they were certainly to be expected in an area of such military significance. These gentlemen, however, were definitely unusual: they spoke

English with a foreign accent – an American, Canadian or possibly even an Australian one.

Their uniforms were unlike others that I had previously seen. Since the time of the Dunkirk evacuation, I had heard foreign accents and seen the uniforms of military people from abroad but the appearance of these men and the way that they spoke, was new to me. I was looking curiously at one of the men, when he suddenly turned around and looked at me.

"What's wrong?" he asked.

I replied, apologetically, "I was just trying to make you out."

"We're doing that all the time, round here," said the other, jesting.

"No, I mean your accent. Are you from New Zealand?" I asked, proud of myself for thinking of another English-speaking country but then immediately feeling foolish for suggesting the one that was probably the least likely.

"No, we're not from there," they said, laughing a little.

"You're Americans, aren't you?" suggested Rosa, whose face lit up with an expression of inordinate joy when her thoughts were confirmed by the smiling, dashing, young, dark-haired warrior to whom she had wasted no time moving closest.

The man seemed considerably delighted as well, after having been identified so positively by my companion. As I reflected upon not having suggested the same nationality myself first, I felt especially foolish when the 'soldier' offered Rosa part of a chocolate bar as a reward.

"There you go, princess," he said, handing her a luxury of which we had seen so very little over the previous few years.

Rosa wasted no time in accepting the gift and instantly began eating it. After a few seconds, she noticed Alun and me enviously staring back at her. She looked a little guilty and immediately offered us a piece each but, just then, the American broke his remaining bar of chocolate in half and gave each of us a portion.

The taste was a pleasure that we had not enjoyed for some considerable time. We gratefully accepted the gifts and – like the 'princess' – consumed the treats as thoroughly and as carefully as possible in order to maximise the duration and effects of the precious, soft, dark, sweet, silky substance.

"Mmm," we all said as we finished carefully licking the last remnants of the delicacies from our lips.

I found it surprising, meritorious and very attractive that the American's pocket should have been so capable of immediately producing such confectionery and in such a quantity. It seemed to delight the Americans, as well, that their generosity was so well received and enthusiastically consumed.

"You haven't had much chocolate recently, have you?" they asked.

"No," was the obvious answer.

We explained how the rationing of it – to a few ounces a month – had turned our previous occasional intake of chocolate into a rare extravagance. Since my time with Mr and Mrs Morgan, we only had it when their children came home on holiday from boarding school. Then, the rations, which had been saved up since the previous holiday, would all be used at once in a gloriously gluttonous extravaganza. Afterwards, we avoided eating or drinking anything else for as long as possible in order to perpetuate the taste of the chocolate in our mouths.

The Americans looked at us with perceptible commiseration but said nothing.

"We've gotta go now," said one of the Americans.

"Where are you off to?" asked Rosa, sadly.

"Into town, then it's back here later."

Rosa, looking a little upset, enquired, "What do you do here?"

"He flies one of those things," said the other American, who pointed at one of the smaller flying boats, each of which had a large, white star conspicuously painted on its side.

"You're a pilot!" exclaimed Rosa, highly impressed.

"What do you do?" Alun asked the other American.

"I navigate," he said, pointing at a badge on his uniform that, I presumed, signified that duty. "I tell him where to go... and which way to come back."

"Will you be flying today?" Alun asked.

"Not today," was the satisfied response.

"When?" Alun persisted, wanting to know more.

The airman paused for a couple of seconds and then said, "Now you know we can't tell you. Don't you, lad? Careless talk costs lives... and all that."

"What are your names?" asked Rosa.

"Clark," said the pilot.

"Douglas," said his navigator.

"I'm Rosa," added my friend who was close to the pilot.

Alun and I mentioned our names as well to the aviators, who shook our hands with a gentle formality.

"Don't worry about those other ships," said Douglas, remembering our concern for the aircraft that had just taken off.

"Other *ships?*" asked Alun, who thought for a few seconds. "Do you mean aeroplanes?"

"Yeah, aeroplanes," Clark confirmed, with a sense of casual authority.

"They all do it... do it all the time. They only take off like that to scare the visitors." Douglas smiled as he said it.

Alun looked at the aircraft in the harbour and, turning to Clark, asked, "Do you take off like that?"

The two Americans looked at each other. Their expressions

suddenly became awkward for a moment, as though they had just suffered a mild personal affront. Clark, to the amusement of Douglas, then stretched out his hand to help illustrate the usual chain of events regarding their take-offs.

"We start the engines, you see. They purr... 'Purr... purr'... and gently... ever so gently like... like a giant floating... feather on the water out there, we glide along... the graceful, silver lines of the *Sally B*..."

"What's the *Sally B*?" enquired Alun, interrupting.

Douglas began to explain: "It's what we named our plane... after –"

Clark now interjected: "My mother," then he continued. "We glide the *Sally B* along on the glassy, rippling, blue water like a... like a..."

"Swan?" I suggested.

"Yes, that's it! Like a swan..." Clark agreed. "The elevators, the flaps... up and down... or down and up, one way or t' other... if at first you don't succeed, and all that. And we skip and we bounce upon the rising waves and then up!

"The fresh spray comes up as well... follows us; the mists of a white haze rise as we rise. And we rise serenely... sedately; journey up higher... gliding almost... floating like... like a giant..."

"Balloon!" Rosa blurted out.

"Balloon..." continued Clark, "... in the gentle breeze... in the drifting, friendly following wind that takes us under its wing... under our wings; that helps us and guides us on our way – not that we've ever needed it much..."

"At all," interjected Douglas.

"Much..." continued Clark, "... and we enter the wide, heavenly domain of the great, white, fluffy clouds and the expanse of an infinite blue yonder... pass the hours passing between each; beneath a golden, bright sun in the warm, silvery... silvery, graceful presence of my lady: majestic... *beautiful Sally B*."

Clark paused for a second or two with his hand up in the air, seeming momentarily lost in a world of his own. Then, self-consciously, he brought it down to his side.

"Say, kids, how 'bout telling us which town you live in?" he suggested. "If one of our missions ever takes us near there and we see you on a hill, I'll bank my wings back and forth..." he illustrated the manoeuvre with his ever-expressive hand, "... so you'll know it's us."

"Could you really do that?" asked Alun.

"Sure, and you be sure to wave back, you hear?"

"We will," promised Rosa.

Alun dutifully explained that we had travelled from Tenby, and drew a rudimentary map of the coastline to assist the Americans in their possible future search for us.

I doubted that such a rendezvous would ever take place but I had nothing to lose by believing that it could happen and I knew that it would be a treat for us children if it did, so I happily went along with the idea. It might also have been a cheery comfort for Douglas and Clark, to know that we children might occasionally have been thinking about them as we watched their perilous flights out or witnessed their fortunate returns. That seemed quite appropriate when, after all, they were undertaking their dangerous missions for us and so many others like us.

As they were leaving, they said that they would see us around but I said that they would most likely not be seeing us around, as we would probably not be going back to the docks for a long time. We thanked the two airmen once more for the gift of their chocolate and all said our goodbyes before we watched the pair confidently stroll down towards the town, where we lost sight of them.

We got some fish and chips and then found a place by the docks to sit for a couple of hours. While we relaxed and chatted, we watched a small boat occasionally moving about and saw another aircraft landing – a return to the harbour that was perfectly executed.

We knew that we had quite a long and exhausting journey home, so we tried resting as much as possible; however, we left in plenty of time to ensure that we would get home while it was still daylight. We wanted to avoid the extra hazard of trying to negotiate the many winding, unlit roads in the dark – a task made extra difficult now because many of the road signs had been removed in order to hamper the progress of any invading Germans.

Too fast... T-O-O F-A-S-T-!

One day, I went cycling with Maggie. We were encouraged to reach the summits of the many steep hills that surround the Tenby district, by knowing that an exhilarating free-wheeling ride down the other side of them always awaited us sooner or later.

I remember that I was going ahead of Maggie as my bike rapidly gained speed down a particularly steep gradient. Suddenly, to my horror, I realized that it was becoming an effort just trying to hold onto the handlebars. At the bottom, disconcertingly, lay a narrow bridge across a small river. As

if that was not enough to worry about, I then perceived a huge lorry making its way towards me from the other side of the bridge!

I considered turning down another lane – away from the bridge and the advancing lorry – but I soon realised that that option was not possible for there *was* no other lane. However, my speed was becoming so great that it precluded that opportunity for salvation anyway – any sharp turns at that point would have been immediately catastrophic. I soon discounted the idea of leaping from my bicycle; it would have been suicidal or, at best, only a way of bringing serious injury to myself that much sooner. As my bike's speed increased, I tried pulling the brake levers harder but their slowing effects were negligible and they only seemed to make the bicycle wobble and shake more, the harder I pulled.

My hill was quickly disappearing, and as the great lorry began to enter the bridge and rapidly fill my vision, I surrendered myself to my expected rather-gruesome fate. The increasing fear that I had, now drenched me in its totality. I let out a final cry, and yet, as I embraced the moment in all of its impending horror, a deep calmness momentarily came over me; I instinctively closed my eyes to the world and left behind all consciousness.

A minute or so later, I opened my eyes and found myself staring up at the biggest rubber wheel that I had ever seen. My elbow was resting against it. Apparently, the lorry had braked when I was about to collide with it.

When I was taken home after the accident, I met the lorry driver, who had been given tea in our house. I was left feeling extremely fortunate when he said that he had had new brakes fitted into the vehicle only that very morning. If he had delayed the replacing of the brakes for another day, the lorry's wheel would almost certainly not have just cut into my elbow a small amount but, instead, would have continued right over me!

More Americans

As the months passed, large numbers of American soldiers started arriving, to be stationed in Tenby or the surrounding areas. Their large quantities of impressive combat paraphernalia struggled to negotiate its way through our town's narrow streets. As they began to outnumber the modest quantity of other foreign Allied fighters in our area, so the terrible fear of a major German invasion of this country finally began to recede with an air of certainty. In its place came a belief – an ever-greater assurance – that victory for the Allied cause would eventually come.

With that, I became more aware of how my presence in Tenby would no longer be necessary – I could return home – although whether the Morgans would immediately demand that I should, was a little uncertain. However, all of that was still far in the future. I had no need to worry about what was going to happen or what I would do, until much nearer that time.

Of the two Americans whom we met originally at the docks – Clark and Douglas – we never did see them or their aircraft again. If we heard someone flying overhead, we often waved to the crew, although I think that none was ever low enough to see us. We certainly saw nothing unusual to attract our attention – like an aircraft banking back and forth to 'wave' its wings, which Clark promised that he would do if he ever saw us waving.

Perhaps our aviator friends – the first of many Americans we were to encounter – left us to join their fellow countrymen who were fighting the Japanese in the Far East. Whatever their fate was, unfortunately, we were not to discover it.

19

The passing years

Christmas

CHRISTMASES IN TENBY were usually predictable, as were the presents. The radio was put on for the first time that year – and it would soon be switched off again for the last. All of the other evacuees and I would congregate in the drawing room to receive presents of books, gloves and other items.

However, one Christmas was quite exceptional, as I received a silver brooch from Mrs Morgan's friend, Lady Evans. Maggie received one with coloured stones. The generous gifts were quite enchanting – both were welcome extravagances that seemed to leave everyone impressed.

The stand-in preacher and the stand-in teacher

Miss Dickinson used to visit small country churches as a stand-in preacher. On several occasions, she took me along as a soloist singer. One comely church that I began visiting, soon after I arrived in Tenby, was at Saundersfoot.

After the services, Miss Dickinson and I would be invited to a certain parishioner's house (although, with its very modest dimensions, it was more like a cottage). We had a meal there, in a room that was small. The medium, oblong dining table was covered with a lace tablecloth, and a highly polished cabinet was also in the room. The furniture appeared small and sparse. The novelty, however, made it a happy occasion.

In the latter period of my time with the Morgans, I became

a stand-in Sunday school teacher. This was pleasurable, as I could tell stories of the type that I found interesting to the smaller children.

Replacements for the servants

When I was fifteen, several changes took place. Because Mrs Morgan's youngest child, Ray, no longer needed a nanny, it was decided to keep only a maid in the house. *I* was then given the job of cleaning the brass on the street door and the step every day, before going to school.

On Saturdays, the passage in the house and the shop floor were washed by Maggie and me. Miss Dickinson always found fault with my work and particularly delighted in moving the heavy oak furniture for me to do it again. The more I protested about it, the more jobs she gave me.

Next, I was given the multicoloured carpet on the stairs to clean with a dustpan and brush. I first had to sprinkle it with dried tea-leaves. Other duties that we had to undertake on Saturdays were the cleaning of the silver cutlery and the dry-cleaning of our tunics.

We also helped with the washing-up.

The piano

Miss Dickinson, being an accomplished piano player, was able to give music lessons. When Ray was approximately five years of age, she too was given piano lessons, starting with the scales. However, I – not being part of their family – was told not to touch the piano, except to dust it; only Mrs Morgan's children and Miss Dickinson were allowed to use it.

There came a time, however, when I was alone in the house. Visits to the cinema only took place when the Morgans' children were home and, during one of those holidays, I was invited to go with them. I politely declined the offer, so they went to the local cinema without me and just took their children and the other evacuees. Without even the maid in the house, who had time off, it occurred to me that it was an ideal time to play the piano.

I rushed into the drawing room, where it was, and raised the polished lid. I thought of a tune and painstakingly found and memorized each note. I was so astounded and proud of my success at this, that I went and opened the bay windows to let the sounds drift outside.

On glancing out after a further session of playing, my eyes fell on a man's figure below in a white jacket. He had a bewildered look on his face as his gaze met mine. I suddenly realized that he was the owner of the barber's shop next door. He must have been wondering why such unfamiliar music/ sounds were emanating from our house, when the normal classical tones or scales were usually played. Horror and reality suddenly gripped me as I hastily withdrew and closed the windows. A word from him to Mrs Morgan regarding this could have entailed a punishment for me. On this occasion, fortunately, I was not found out.

Final eisteddfod... and exams

After the passage of several years, I entered my school's eisteddfod singing contest for the last time. Once more, I was one of three girl soloists. Each of us represented our own particular house in the school. My closest rival – a girl with a considerable talent for exercising her vocals – was again Sheila Hurd.

Each of us singers delivered an emotional rendition to our attentive audience as though some leading role in a West End or Broadway production depended upon it. If ever there appeared desperation in our performances, it was only to beat the others – to be the eventual victor.

At the end of the closely fought competition, the losers departed with notable grace. The house of Tudor finished the day with its third victory in four years.

School, of course – even a Welsh one – was not just about

singing; there were exams to be taken as well. Mr Morgan encouraged me to stay for another year – beyond the legal age requirement of fourteen, when I could have left. The school, proud of its pupils' achievements, also did its best to strongly encourage everyone to remain for the final examinations.

In July, I undertook each of them, sitting in silence in the school hall. The results of those School Certificate Examinations were very pleasing for me. I had passes in History and Mathematics, and credits in English Language, English Literature, Scripture Knowledge, French (written and oral), Art and Arithmetic. I was particularly good at French, eventually coming top in the subject.

I walked past the school gates for the last time after having achieved far more at the school than I had originally expected. The awkwardness of being an evacuee – an outsider, like many before and after me – had not been allowed to cause me failure.

Other pupils, from stable family backgrounds, almost seemed guaranteed success. I was encouraged – by Mr Morgan, especially – to understand that I was just as good as the next person. I proved him right when I left school having achieved qualifications that were as good as those of my contemporaries.

First kiss

We evacuees in the Morgans' house eagerly awaited the return of their children from boarding school. We particularly wanted to see Alun again, for he tended to be a bit of a charmer! We wondered whom he would flirt with. Each of us hoped that we would be the one, which usually caused a bit of a competition to develop among us, as we each tried to make ourselves look especially pretty just before he came. The other girls had curly hair and attractive faces, so I felt at a disadvantage.

It was with some surprise then, that Alun asked if *I*

would like to take a walk with him along the beach and see the monastery. I gladly agreed. We both left the house and proceeded to walk along the esplanade and then on to the beach. It was a summer's evening. The tide was out and very few people were about. He spoke little and I despaired of ever seeing the monastery, as it was a long way off.

Suddenly, he pushed me down onto a sand dune. I then felt a warm mouth on mine. Immediately after, he pulled me to my feet. We continued walking as if nothing had happened. It had been my first kiss from a male and I was bemused by it. Neither of us ever spoke about it, so I put it down to the romantic setting that we encountered and thought that, perhaps, I was not so unattractive after all!

The war

In the middle of 1944, the many troops who had been arriving in great numbers for the previous few months suddenly departed for the beaches of Normandy, to clear France and the Low Countries of the Germans – to begin the end of the Second World War.

It was then that my mother wrote to me, stating that she had changed her address from Weston Rise in London to Affleck Street, only a few hundred yards along. Meanwhile, her mother – my grandmother – remained close to her in Pentonville Road.

I initially thought that it was strange that she had suddenly found a reason to move but my curiosity quickly waned when, in the same letter, she informed me of the very sad news of the death of our friend: the amiable Mr Bridge. His demise was through a secret weapon of Hitler's – the V-1, which stood for Reprisal Weapon One – although what exactly Mr Bridge had done, for which Hitler was seeking revenge, went far beyond my capacity to understand.

I paused for a moment to remember earlier times. I realised that I was going to do no more errands for Mr

Bridge. I would never again see the smiling, welcoming face of his. No more would I hear his "Thank you, Lily" or get any more pennies from him in gratitude for a job well done. I never even said goodbye to him.

Alas, I bid you goodbye now then, Mr Bridge.

A little while later, I realised that my mother was lucky not to have been killed instead of – or as well as – Mr Bridge. Her living in such close proximity to him, meant that she was probably not far from the explosion that killed him.

Now a new brother to return to...

A short while later, my mother sent another letter, informing me of the birth of my new brother, John. Once again, she was not forthcoming about the father's name.

The redistribution of wealth

Apart from keeping me informed of her change of address and other events, my mother also occasionally sent me some money. However, the Morgans felt that they were entitled to it and secretly just kept it from me.

After a while I realized what was happening, so, feeling that 'all's fair in love and war', I decided to beat them at their own game. When I was working in the shop, I might sometimes have sold something for a shilling, for example, but instead of putting the money in the shop till, I would just pocket it. Thus, over a period of time, I recouped the money that was owed to me.

I assumed that Maggie – who regularly helped in the shop as well – was also having some of her money misappropriated, as she would also keep some of the money from sales, for herself!

20

Changes

A new perspective

ONE DAY, WHEN I happened to be walking along the passage in the house, I encountered Mr and Mrs Morgan and Miss Dickinson huddled together. The conversation was animated. Important conversations usually took place in the drawing room or bedrooms – out of earshot of us evacuees – but they were so overwrought by the matter that involved them, they did not care who in the house would hear them. I pricked up my ears on passing.

"Can't you get the lease extended?" was Mrs Morgan's shrill cry.

"I've tried that!" was Mr Morgan's response.

"What about the children?" interrupted Miss Dickinson.

I realised they faced a serious situation regarding the house and wondered about the outcome – especially when 'the children' were possibly going to be facing some sort of upheaval in the near future.

A few days later, I found them together again in the same place, only this time they sounded exhilarated.

"Will I have to go to London?" queried Mrs Morgan.

"Of course," replied Mr Morgan.

This time the conversation revolved around the award of a BEM to Mrs Morgan, for taking in so many evacuees – the five of us children who had been with her for years and a few others who had stayed for shorter periods. When she eventually gave us a glimpse of her medal, her delight was plain to see.

Not long afterwards, when having a meal in the kitchen, Mr Morgan informed us that we would be moving to a different part of the town. It then came about, within a few weeks, that we were taken by Mr Morgan to view the new home.

We walked along several streets until we came to the promenade that had many hotels facing the sea. We went a little farther until we came to the largest one. This had two entrances and looked very imposing.

Mr Morgan suddenly stopped and said, "In you all go."

We hesitated, somewhat overawed, and then did as he bade. On this visit, we waited in the lounge while he finalized arrangements in another room.

In the hotel, there were four floors – covered with expensive Indian carpets – and a basement. On moving in, Mrs Morgan indicated that we would be sleeping in the small rooms on the top floor. The guests had the two floors below and on the ground floor there was a lounge and a large dining room with individual small, round tables, each holding small vases of flowers.

The two small rooms alongside the dining room were taken over by Miss Dickinson and Mrs Morgan, who used them for reception and office purposes. The basement was in stark contrast to the elegant upstairs rooms. The extremely large, square-shaped kitchen had a grey-stone floor and very large windows with no curtains. It appeared very drab and incorporated large, black ovens and a very large, old wooden table.

The bedroom that I was given was small, with a round porthole type of window that offered only a limited view of the coastal scenery. There was a single bed and chest of drawers with a mirror placed on it and a long, narrow cupboard. I found it depressing.

The new maid

At the beginning of our time in the hotel, we all helped to complete the many various duties that enabled the place to function properly – even Mr Morgan was now laying the tables for guests, which looked very odd, as it somewhat gave him the appearance of a waiter. However, as time went on, I found myself helping to make the beds for the guests and tidying their rooms.

When confronted with a bedroom that had clothes strewn across the floor and articles attached to knobs, I called to the maid who was with me, "What on earth has been going on in here?"

She smiled and replied sardonically, "Oh, that's the way of the rich guests – the richer they are, the more they expect from you." There was a resignation in her voice. I surveyed the mess and decided that the way of life there was worse than before.

The staff who were originally working in the hotel gradually left. The cook was the last to go. Mrs Morgan said she did not like her because she had different ideas about what the menus should contain, and the food was too expensive anyway.

The Morgans employed a married couple instead. As well as food preparation, they were given other duties. That resulted in me being frequently asked to go on errands for them. To me, they were worse than the previous cook was, as their frequent mistakes caused friction with the guests when incorrect menus were done. Mr Morgan had the job of placating the unfortunate diners when this happened.

It was a time of great excitement when the first of our guests arrived, who, incidentally, was a captain. We fussed around him quite a lot and wondered who would arrive next and what they would want.

Well-rehearsed routines went into operation to ensure that events ran smoothly or were there to cater for the unexpected little disasters. As time went on, however, the workload increased, the novelty value decreased and it all became far less exciting.

The clandestine prisoners of war operation
I was now sixteen and friendly with Lowri, who had been at the other residence. She was a few years older than I was.

We had become friends when I accompanied her to her home in a village, a few miles away; her mother had just died. Her father wanted her to leave her position as maid, as he felt lonely in his large house. She decided against this but promised that she would visit him when she had her leave.

"I have met two Italian prisoners of war who work on a farm," she said one day. "They are staying here and not going back. They asked if I would go out with them tonight and bring a friend. Would you be interested?" she queried.

The chance to escape a dull routine and make a decision independently seemed overwhelmingly attractive. However, I did not think that it was possible.

"I'll be missed," I stated.

"No you won't," she quickly replied.

We then agreed a plan, an important part of which was to exploit a feature of the hotel's design: the fact that it had two entrances. I was to say good night to Mr and Mrs Morgan and appear to go to bed but, without them knowing, I was to slip out of the least-used entrance, which was at the far end of the hotel.

Later that day, I did as we had decided and pretended to go to my room but sneaked down the stairs instead. I held my breath while making my way down them; I was annoyed that there were so many and apprehensive in case I was caught. I eventually arrived outside, where Lowri was standing beside the door, waiting for me.

We hurried along the pathway in the semi-darkness,

struggling to avoid the bushes and small trees that lined our way on either side of us and whose various waving, extended branches seemed desperate to grab hold of us, to catch our clothes, legs and arms and never let us go. We prevailed over the life of the garden, leaving its hindrance behind as we travelled deeper into dark, unexplored territory.

As we made our way to the top of the nearby cliff – which was several hundred yards from the hotel – I caught sight of two dark-haired men. Their faces were tanned and they were casually dressed. In the distance, they appeared to be short. As we approached them, I discovered that they really were quite short!

Before I could speak, Lowri went up to them and introduced me. We had made a plan, before meeting them, that we would keep each other in sight, as a precaution. The taller one, with brown eyes and a ready tongue, took Lowri's hand and walked quickly away. The one left, stood facing me.

"Would you like to take a walk?" he asked, with a smile.

I agreed. I pointed in the direction where Lowri had gone. After walking a short distance along the isolated cliff top, we sat down. His command of English seemed limited and there was an awkward silence. It was at this point that I noticed Lowri running along towards me.

She grabbed my hand and bade the astounded Italian I was with goodbye! She did not speak further until he was out of sight. She was agitated as she spoke.

"I don't know what his idea of a night out is, but it's different to mine. I thought I'd better warn you as to what they're like." She looked totally disillusioned. "How was your one?" she added as an afterthought.

I smiled slowly and said, "You'll never know!" I could not resist the remark.

End game
(Dramatization)

Nazi Germany surrendered in May 1945. VE Day – Victory in Europe Day – was made a national holiday in celebration. Rows of red, white and blue bunting – hanging along washing lines – criss-crossed above the roads. Union flags proudly fluttered from windows or hung on small, improvised flagpoles. Outdoor parties were organized, where children sat behind lines of tables and ate precious food rations that had been expectantly saved up in the preceding weeks specially for the occasion.

In the late afternoon, a fancy-dress parade was held along the high street. Many people dressed up as famous contemporary military or political celebrities. A military band marched past playing martial music to raise our spirits even higher. Everywhere was gaily decorated; all sights and sounds promoted an unforgettable occasion.

In the evening, we had the radio on specially to hear King George talk to the nation about our victory. Outside, there were songs from throngs, including the national anthem. On the hill above the harbour, a pile of wood, rags and other inflammable rubbish was built. Upon it was placed a dummy representing Hitler. Its appearance included drawn-on facial features, a stuck-on moustache and – upon its arm – the symbolic black swastika.

As darkness fell, the pyre was lit. We stood back and watched with unrestrained joy and relief as the German dictator's image was slowly consumed by the hot, flickering flames; as in hell, it burned. With the cheers of all and the occasional colourful language of some, we expressed pride in our nation's final victory, and hostility towards the erstwhile Nazi regime. Even the little boats in the harbour below joined in; they accompanied all with their enthusiastic sirens and horn blasts.

Being by the coast, we had been forced to keep our

unpleasant black-out precautions until the very end of the war in Europe. Now, with no enemy nearby from whom we had to hide, that troublesome period came to an abrupt and welcome end. Lights at night were to remain bright everywhere from now on.

To many of the people who had been temporarily placed in Tenby for their own safety during the war, the flames warmed their souls; the illuminations – beacons – directed their thoughts; and those thoughts, inevitably, were soon to turn to home.

Nancy

Nancy had been about to complete her junior school education and then go back to London, when my mother – without a clear explanation – advised Nancy to remain in Tenby. Now, with the war in Europe over, Nancy was told to finish her first year at her new school and then return home during the forthcoming summer holidays.

I wanted to return with Nancy but I was now a young adult and somewhat the master of my own destiny and thought it wrong to become another burden for my mother, even for a while. I knew, therefore, that Nancy and I would have to part soon. However, at the start of her holidays, we took a little time to do a bit more travelling around Tenby together while we still could.

Contemplation
(Dramatization)

The summer holidays came and went. One evening, in search of solitude, I left the hotel by myself and went down to the seashore.

The beach was quiet. The sun was low down. A slow breeze passed me by. Soft, cool, wet sand oozed easily between my toes. A trail of my footprints snaked wildly behind me. The tide was in retreat; the shore of shallow channels and isolated pools of seawater lay prostrate before my presence.

The giant Goscar Rock that almost claimed my life years before, when I dived from it, sat ahead of me upon its rippled, golden-brown carpet. When the sea had disguised the form's true dimensions, it was empowered to lure the naïve to the quiet deep. Now, deserted by its deadly accomplice, it was calm and quite unthreatening. I leant forward and touched the foot of it; it was cold.

I scaled it and reached the summit – with relative ease compared to my first attempt, years before. Staring into the distance, I watched storm clouds form on the horizon and the failing sun turn her back on me. The beclouded landscape chilled. There was no one else on the beach as far as I could see. A breeze passed through my clothes and I shivered a little.

I embraced the moment on high, the opportunity to be like some warrior queen – a Boudicca or grand Britannia in command at the top of her world. I pointed my arm before me and called upon the sea to stay back and the storm clouds to abate. A final act of theatre, with an audience of one, played itself out with the same success as an edict of tidal refrain from King Cnut. The sea proved irresistible. The storm, angered by the challenge to its authority, advanced unhesitatingly; redoubling its strength, its darkness, depth and its threat.

I waited an hour – possibly two – for the tide to return. As it inexorably crept closer, I came down from the rock and ascended to a higher peak. There I stood and looked around, atop a desolate, grassy summit. I walked along a little and then sat down on a patch of soft grass as my thoughts turned to home and the family I was missing. I wanted to see Nancy, who had gone back to London, and Doris, who – I assumed – had already returned home. I wanted to be with my mother again and meet my new brother and sister – John and Joan. I was sure that they were all now happily getting used to a normal way of life. They were all in their new property – together; meanwhile, I was living once more without any personal relatives.

The sea below was beginning to lose its composure. The dark, menacing clouds continued to form above it. I stood up and viewed them stretching from horizon to horizon. They dwarfed this insignificant soul, standing alone on the cliff. The awesome situation continued to develop.

Self-confidence, money and freedom, and the great cost of the rail fare home: of those, I thought much. I reflected upon an impetuous youth, unwelcome advances and the shadow of over-possessiveness. I felt caged within a cauldron of relationships; what forms them, what thwarts them and a concern that was lacking for the consequences of both – all now weighed heavily upon my mind. I bemoaned the fear to express spirit. I did not know which way to turn – depression was my only bearing.

The blackening sky began to sprinkle fine droplets gently upon me. A tear from a breaking heart came to my eye and passed down my cheek. I felt so alone, just as my sister,

Doris, must have felt at the farm when I left her many years before. I relearned the act of lamentation.

"Que sera sera – Whatever will be, will be," my mother spoke to me. "Take each day as it comes. All things work out for the best in the long run. To thyself be true."

They were my favourite mottoes; my mother was always using them. They comforted me now, spoke to me of my future, and – for a few moments – they stopped me worrying about it.

The unrestricted, penetrating cold wind, increasing all the while, was becoming a force requiring a considerable effort to counter – when I countenanced not being carried along with it. Curtains of rain passed in undulating sheets before me; a violent downpour appeared to be in the offing. I was about to be drenched in water, frightened with a thunderclap or even slain in an instant with a bolt of lightning. I was near no shelter, yet – surrendering to a capricious nature – I did not care for any.

In the distance, shafts of bright, white sunbeams broke through the eclipse of boiling, grey clouds. The spreading, translucent fingers assuredly parted the expansive storm and rested their emboldening tips upon the troubled water. A tiny, solitary rock – fighting its own desperate little battle to stay above the waves – appeared to take courage from the radiant intervention. It sat proud and illuminated for a few minutes, while the lights of the heavenly image slowly moved around it, reflecting a nature in perpetual conflict in that quarter of a restless sea.

The struggle for enlightenment was never-ending, though. The spirit persisted for a while before fading away – overcome as quickly as it had been reborn. But if the sun was dying, it doubtless was to return another day in that grand, yet obscure, scheme of things. Brilliant and triumphant would surely be its indomitable presence – tomorrow or the day after that, or soon.

And in that cheerless time of such abstruse contemplation, I took heart as I heard my mother gently say once more to me: "Que sera sera."

21

The beginning of the end

Resolution

WHEN SITTING ALONE in my bedroom and gazing out of the window, I thought about my life in Tenby, and my future. I thought about where I had lived – on a farm, in a mansion, in the Morgans' house and now at the top of their grand hotel – and where I wanted to live. Despite the changing physical point of view, nothing had altered my emotional one – my innate sense of belonging.

Upon the reflection grew the countenance of one more change; I yearned for another place and that was London. I felt more confident than at any time previously. I was sixteen and wanted to be in charge of my own destiny. It was autumn 1945. The war was over; there was no reason for me to stay.

As I made the decision to go, I realized that that was the easy part. Telling the Morgans was going to be harder. I plucked up my courage and went downstairs. Mrs Morgan was leaving her room.

She smiled and I faltered as I said, "I've something to tell you." She saw that I looked apprehensive and took me into her office. I then added, "I want to go."

"Go where?" was the reply.

"To London," I countered, swiftly.

At that, she closed her door and proceeded to lecture me on all of the reasons why she thought that it was best for me to remain in Tenby. After about an hour, she opened her door and directed me towards Miss Dickinson's room. She was not there, which gave me time to think up answers to the inevitable questions.

Different strategies were used to try to make me change my mind. I was reminded how 'fortunate' I was to be living in a place like theirs, in Tenby, rather than in the far more 'depressing' surroundings of my family's home, back in London.

I held my ground and made the final statement, which she could not refute: "The war is over!"

There was silence and then she asked when I was going.

"Tomorrow," I said.

She looked in disbelief. "You've no fare money."

I turned to her and said that I had. Months earlier, Miss Dickinson and I had spent the evening walking through the town unbeknown to Mrs Morgan, who was out. We were crossing the road and as I was about to step on the pavement, I saw a sum of money – a bundle of notes screwed up on the kerb. We were outside the church, which was the other side of where we had previously lived.

Miss Dickinson suggested that I should I take the money to the police station because, if it was not claimed within six months, I could have it. I went to the station, filled in a form as required and noted the date.

I eventually collected the money, as it was not claimed. Maggie advised me to use it to go home. It was the exact amount, to the penny, for the fair back to Kings Cross. Until this penultimate day with the Morgans, I had kept its purpose a secret from the family, as advised.

When Miss Dickinson did eventually turn up, to add her opinion to the altercation, her final words spoken were loud, shrill and threatening: "You'll regret it… you'll see! You'll regret it!"

As she repeated the words, I strode away. Fear suddenly gripped me as to the future. The break had been made. I was on my own from now on. I walked blindly towards the stairs. Suddenly, Mrs Morgan caught my arm; her manner had changed.

"You can't leave like this. I'll get Gly to go with you to the train in the morning. I'll help you pack your clothes."

I turned and looked at her. She looked calm and hurt. I could see that she did not wish me to leave on bad – or perhaps on any – terms. I steeled myself and knew that to back out now would be to stay forever. I was resolved to overcome all obstacles and go home.

The morning came.

"Will you change your mind?" Mrs Morgan pleaded as I stood with my cases, ready to go.

I ignored the question and kissed them all goodbye, except Gly, who stood waiting to go to the station with me.

The walk down the roads was quiet. The farewell to Gly at the station was short, as the train had arrived early. I took the large case that she was carrying and thanked her. As I stared at her grim face, I suddenly remembered that she was the one who had been there to meet me when I had first arrived in Tenby, all those years ago.

She had appeared bossy and spoilt then. However, she had been there to save my life on one occasion and the holidays spent with her and her siblings had made life bearable. She had become a good friend and it seemed right for her to be there with me, at the end. It was now the conclusion of seeing, at firsthand, how different life was for the middle classes.

A cold wind suddenly caught Gly's long, woollen scarf, which she had to adjust. I surveyed the scene before me: we were standing on a narrow platform with only a few people about. It did not seem possible that I would never see Gly again.

"You'll find it's all changed," she murmured.

Fear struck me then, as I had always thought of London as staying the way it was when I left it.

"Maybe," I said laconically, "but my home is there. It's where I belong." A sudden surge of pride welled in me. My eyes filled with tears. The war had brought us together; its end was now driving us apart.

I stepped into the train, put my belongings on a rack and wound down the window. I looked at Gly's forlorn figure as the train started to pull slowly out of the station, and waved. We were never to see each other again.

22

An end and a new beginning

The world that I returned to

AN ENDURING INDUSTRY, and housing that was chock-a-block, and bomb-sites – frequent bomb-sites – greeted my return to the indomitable capital. When my train eventually stopped at the station, I took my suitcase and made my way out to the street, where the cacophony of shouts and bustling crowds reminded me that I had bought my independence at the cost of the beautiful sights of Tenby. There I was, in London. I had 'made it'.

It did not take me long to find my mother's home, which she had moved to a year earlier. Hers was a tenement house, one of several terraced and next door to a pub. I climbed up the steps to the front door. Below me were the windows of a basement. Ahead and above, were three more floors. I put my suitcase down, breathed an exhausted sigh of relief and knocked on the door.

Nothing happened for a few seconds. All sorts of thoughts quickly flashed through my mind. I contemplated the consequences of something having caused my family not to be there. If they were not, I wondered how I would find them and where I would live. I certainly could not return to the Morgans, not after showing such determination to get away from them.

Suddenly, someone approached the door from the other side. I breathed my second exhausted sigh of relief and prepared myself to greet my mother after five long years away. The door catch unlocked, the heavy door opened and now all of my fears and insecurities were to be assuaged by... someone else!

I was stunned and confused at the same time. Before me stood a rather slim woman, aged about thirty, who was definitely not my mother. Through one of the doorways inside, I saw a couple of children – who were not my siblings – playing. It was as though the fears that I had had only moments earlier were now, frighteningly, coming true.

"I'm looking for Mrs Smith," I explained, hoping for a positive response but not altogether expecting to hear anything good. The woman looked at my appearance quite closely, which made me a little nervous. "I'm her daughter. I've come to live with her. She wrote to me and said that she was living here."

"Oh, they're upstairs," said the woman suddenly, to my enormous relief, and then she wasted no time leading me up to the landing on the first floor, where the Smith's portion of the house began. "This floor's yours and you've got all the upstairs as well. That's the toilet there, though, and I'm afraid we all share that. I'm Mrs Richards. If you need something, you know where I am. I'm down there," she said, helpfully pointing at the floors below.

"We're neighbours now, so we've got to stick together, haven't we? Where are you from?" she probed, inquisitively.

"Wales."

"Wales?" she replied, being somewhat taken aback. "I thought as much, what with your strange accent 'n' all."

What accent was that, I wondered. Then I suddenly realised that it was the strange Welsh one that I had been subtly acquiring over the previous five years. It probably sounded as unusual to her as the local London one now appeared to me.

"What were you doing in Wales?"

"I was evacuated there during the war."

"You were an evacuee?"

"Yes... and I've been away since 1940."

"1940, you say? Well... Still, you're home now, aren't you?"

"Yes," I said. "I'm home now." The phrase struck me with an unexpected sense of deep poignancy.

With that, Mrs Richards left me and went back downstairs. I almost expected her to shout out, when she reached the bottom of the stairs, "I'm down here now!" and start waving to me. I stayed away from the top of the stairs, lest I should have inadvertently given her another excuse to do just that.

I stood quietly on the landing for a minute, listening to the sounds coming from the room beside me. I tried to work out who was saying what, when a distant, familiar voice said, "I wonder what all that commotion was, going on outside."

Before I could properly compose myself or rehearse a speech for my long-awaited dramatic entrance, the door suddenly swung open. There, in the doorway, stood my stunned mother.

"Hoo, hoo, Lily!" she exclaimed, with a voice made high-pitched by the excitement of the moment. She rushed out and hugged me. Her eyes quickly glazed over.

Then others from inside the room – Arthur and Nancy – came out and greeted me, welcoming me back, and quite a hullabaloo began that took several minutes to subside. My new little brother and sister – John and Joan – stood in the background, not quite understanding what all of the fuss was about. I beheld the sight of the two young people with whom I had so much in common, yet had never seen and never known. I crouched down to get more intimate with them and gave them both a big sisterly hug. I started to cry. I had finally returned to my family.

Then I noticed that Doris appeared absent.

"Where's Doris?" I asked. "Is she out playing?"

"She's stayed at the farm," was my mother's curt reply. Her mood changed noticeably.

"The one I was evacuated to?" I enquired further; confused and rather perturbed to say the least.

"Yes," she said.

I persisted with my questions.

"But when is she coming back?"

"She's *not* coming back... She's *never* coming back... Now I don't want to talk about it any more," she snapped.

Immediately changing the subject, she invited me inside our new half of a house, to rest and have some refreshments.

"Come in, Lily... Have a cup of tea. I'll put some food on for you."

I was shocked at the news of Doris. I could not leave the subject of her there but I could see that it was upsetting my mother to talk about it, so I chose my timing carefully before persisting with any more questions. I needed more information about what had happened, if I was to come to terms with Doris' absence – especially if it was to be permanent.

A little while later, my mother explained – somewhat briefly – that when she visited the farm one day, Mr Greenwood asked her if he could adopt my sister, who had been getting on fine with the farming family. After Mr Greenwood had convinced my mother that he would look after the young child well and would spoil her, the adoption process was allowed to proceed.

My mother doubtless thought that she was doing what was best for Doris, whose future now appeared assured – no longer would my sister's life be one of struggle in the household of my mother's, where there were so many other young people to look after. However, Doris' opinion of her adoption had been neither sought nor expressed: her young age left her unable to influence proceedings, even if she had so desired. I, on the other hand, was a little older than Doris was, with a better capacity to express self-will, so I came home and she did not, and never would.

I was upset and could not get out of my mind the idea that I had abandoned Doris and that she might have remained behind because of what I had done. If I had stayed on the farm, I would have been there to take Doris back home, which I presumed she would have wanted. However, under those circumstances, I too might have been adopted!

The only way to assuage my feelings of guilt for what had happened to my sister at the farm, was to remind myself that – within a few weeks of our arrival there – I was driven to return to London in disgust at the killing of the animals. Doris and I were city girls for whom killing was an alien occupation; we did not belong there.

We were told never again to speak about Doris. It hurt me that my sad vision of her, five years before, was to have been my last. The goodbyes that we spoke to each other were not temporary but were to be for all time. From now on, a seemingly innocuous goodbye – especially to a close relative – would have a troubling aura, an echo perhaps, of tainted permanence about it.

What was done out of love, hurt.

Arthur travels and then his father sits on him

My brother, Arthur, relayed to me *his* evacuation stories. After he was evacuated with Doris and me in 1939, he quickly parted company from us and eventually went back to London. When he returned following two more unsuccessful evacuations, my mother gave up trying to send him away and kept him at home.

Around 1943, our father returned to the family for a *final* time. Arthur had only seen him a couple of times before that. On that third occasion, Arthur was sitting on a chair when his dad entered the room and sat on him, hurting my brother's legs!

Such was our 'father'.

The new view

The top floor of our new residence contained the two bedrooms. My sisters shared one; my brothers, the other. My mother slept on a kind of couch in the lounge. Only when the room was vacated, at the end of the day, was she able to go to 'bed'. As I had to sleep somewhere, space was found for me in my sisters' bedroom.

The lounge was, perhaps, ten feet square and contained one long wooden table along the side, and a smaller one in the middle. Two small chairs sat next to the door, and the couch was against the wall. Opposite the door was a coal fire with a single gas light above it. No electricity ran through the house; candles often supplemented the insufficient flickering gas flame at night.

On my first night back home in London, I reopened the curtains of my *new* bedroom window and looked, with some sadness, at what had become of my home city. It was now a picture of a broken landscape – one marked by striking brush strokes and the joyless colours from, perhaps, history's darkest palette.

I bemoaned that such a beautiful canvas should have been so treated, but I drew on the strength that grows from the experience of the most terrible of wars and on the hope, now, of certain recovery, and retired in the satisfaction that all that I held dearest in my life had, at least, survived.

A prisoner of the Japanese

As the days passed, Aunt Eleanor's husband – Uncle Henry – made himself known to me again. Before the war, he had always been outgoing, boisterous and cheerful. I was unaware that, unfortunately, he had been a soldier in the Far East and had suffered much at the hands of the Japanese after they had captured him.

When the war was over and he had returned home – an event for which he felt particularly fortunate – it was clear that he was a broken man. He had become very withdrawn. He was quite thin and had visibly suffered the deterioration of all of his teeth during his detention. He could not be persuaded to tell us of his experiences as a prisoner of the Japanese and certainly never volunteered any information. The memories of what he had endured from his captors were to remain forever locked up and far away in the deepest recesses of his troubled mind.

The site

Within days, my mother took me back to Weston Rise, where I was shocked to behold a line of grey, contorted forms standing defiantly around a vast crater where my house once stood. As I looked before me, I understood most clearly the reason for my mother's move to nearby Affleck Street; and the death of poor Mr Bridge, who had always refused the 'inconvenient' trek into an air-raid shelter, and had been in our house when the Flying Bomb came over. My mother's persistence in sending her children away as evacuees or taking them with her to a shelter might have prevented us suffering the same fate as that that befell Mr Bridge.

Now, my family were rebuilding their lives, albeit from scratch. The house in which we now resided had been loaned – or somewhat requisitioned – from its previous inhabitants. Their need of it was not as great as that of my mother's, who was struggling to look after her many children. The furniture and many other essential items that we were now using were acquired through similar charitable or government-organised emergency means. I think that it was fortunate that we were given such assistance, for I believe that my mother was hardly able to salvage anything from the wreckage of our Weston Rise home. What she could retrieve was put by the council into temporary storage until her new accommodation at Affleck Street could be secured.

Weston Rise was now no more than a playground of rubble and ruins, which told in its own way the story of the time of devastation, of a man-made storm, annihilation... and endurance, and as I looked at it, it put my concerns and troubles of recent months into perspective. I realised that my mother had accepted, most stoically, a substantial upset; I was clearly the daughter of a considerable survivor.

Maggie

After my fellow evacuee, Maggie, had returned home, I kept a promise to meet her again. One day, I took the short walk to her house in Caledonian Road, to see her.

When I arrived, I knocked on the door. Maggie came and opened it, and immediately greeted me with a big smile. She invited me inside and introduced me to her rough-looking parents (although she did not describe them as such). Maggie's appearance was now (inadvertently) looking like that of the character Samantha from the 1960s comedy, *Bewitched*.

The house was sparsely furnished – everywhere emanated a sense of deprivation. The large lounge, for instance, effectively contained just a few benches, which had been placed around the edge. It was an uninviting abode.

Maggie was someone who had been adopted. That depressing existence, to which she had returned, was another sad aspect of her life to date. I could not help hoping that not all adopted children ended up living in miserable situations like the one that I encountered there.

Although they were decent people and they gave me something to eat and drink during my stay there, I did not like their pitiable lifestyle and, unfortunately, I did not feel able to visit them again.

End of adolescence

My family was not what it used to be. I was not the child that I once was. Life was going to be different.

I soon got a job but because I had not been given a typewriter, I left and secured a better position at Nottidges – a large, local department store where I sold women's clothing, curtain materials and other such merchandise.

Around Christmas 1947, I went to a party with work colleagues Doreen and Peggy, and Peggy's friend Kenny. A couple of his male friends were also going.

When we arrived, Doreen said, "He looks nice" but fortunately she was not referring to the good-looking young man whom I immediately fancied. Her eyes were on Derek, who was one of the other men. My interest was directed towards George, who was handsome, brawny and not all that dissimilar to how the actor John Travolta would later appear in the film *Grease*.

At the end of the day, I was escorted home by both George and Kenny, at least until we reached Kenny's home, when George told him that he had no need to escort me any further. When we reached my house, George accompanied me up the stairs, said goodnight to me and, rather disappointingly, just left. I have to admit that I expected at least a little peck on the cheek from my beau after such a long journey home.

A few days later, George returned to my house. Nancy enquired what the purpose of his visit was, and then called out to me to go downstairs, as he had come to ask me if I wanted to go to the cinema with him. My heart lifted for a moment, I hesitated for a second or two and then I happily accepted his invitation, with the only proviso being that he was to give me a couple of minutes to get ready.

Nancy said, "She'll come out. Just wait over on the corner," which was only about three houses away.

A few minutes later, I went downstairs and outside to meet George, who had been patiently awaiting my arrival. I went up to him and put my arm in his, and then the pair of us began our journey down the road for an evening together at the local cinema. As we strolled along, George mentioned that he was somewhat relieved when I approached *him*, because there was another young man standing on the opposite corner to his and he was a little worried in case I would have left the house and gone walking away with the wrong person!

We returned to my house at about eleven o'clock. I invited George inside, where he met my mother for the first time. She was sitting beside the fire and was the only one, apart from us, who was still awake.

George had a cordial chat with her for about half an hour, where he explained a little about his work as a wood machinist and other circumstances, and discovered that my mother was working opposite his business, in Great Ormond Street Children's Hospital, doing some cleaning and polishing. At the end of the proceedings, he went home.

We had now become a courting couple.

23

New life experiences:
the young adult and beyond

The cinemas

VISITS TO THE cinema played a major part in our courting days. A day or so after our first trip there, George invited me back again. There was a great profusion of local ones, including the Empire, the Odeon, the Angel and a particularly big one called the Blue Hall. We went at least four nights a week. Different films were usually shown in different cinemas and each normally changed its presentations weekly.

Neither of our families owned one of the new television sets that were now being produced but even if we did, we would probably still have gone out to see a film because of the privacy that that afforded. So that we would not impolitely spoil other people's views of the screen, we usually sat on the back row, where it was also cosy.

We usually saw two films during the evening. In between the first and the second, there was the evening's Pathé newsreel – a short black and white film narrated by an off-screen man with a sprightly and authoritative voice.

During such presentations, I would often be sucking an orange, munching an apple, eating some other fruit or – best of all – consuming sweets and chocolates. When the intervals came, if I wanted to treat myself further, I would buy a choc-ice from one of the usherettes who walked up and down the aisles. Thus, when the news was on, it could almost be said that the 'sound bites' that the audience heard were coming both from the front *and* the back of the auditorium!

The walks and the Lyons Tea Room

Sometimes in the evenings, instead of seeing a film, we went for a stroll to Hyde Park. Quite often, forthright people would be standing on soap-boxes at Hyde Park Corner and moaning to the public, usually about political issues. The speakers seemed to entertain most people more than they seriously influenced them.

Later, we strolled down Oxford Street and one or two other famous places that were very pleasant. We did not notice the distance that we were travelling, as we enjoyed looking at the various shops as we walked along – and each other!

Some nights, particularly during bad weather, we retreated to the Lyons Tea Room for sandwiches and drinks like cups of tea, which were ideal, as we generally did not drink alcohol. It was a comfortable place and near where I lived.

When we got to my house, often just before midnight, we went into the passageway where we had a little, quiet romantic kiss and cuddle for five or ten minutes. We were careful and made sure that we did not disturb our neighbours in the next room, which was a few yards away, and remained downstairs where we were least likely to encounter my young, curious siblings. After I kissed George goodnight, I made my way upstairs to my room, leaving my gallant beau to find his own way home.

The visitors

One day in 1949, I saw my father, his new partner – who was standing on the stairs – and my sister, Rhona. They were visiting Mrs Richards, a dressmaker, in order to buy a dress.

When Rhona saw me, she asked, "Are you Lilian?"

Perhaps my appearance had changed noticeably during

the nine or ten years in which we had not seen each other and that was why she had difficulty recognising her sister.

"Yes," I replied.

To me, Rhona was like a stranger; we had little in common; we spoke differently. I had nothing to say to her.

The bakery and my brushes with fame

I eventually left Nottidges, to work in a bakery shop in London's Theatre Land – the West End. A few famous actors and actresses shopped there, including Valerie Hobson and – one of my favourite ones – Kay Kendall.

After a while, I got to know them quite well. They often gave me tickets for their theatres. I also received tickets from some of the people who worked behind the scenes on the productions. Thus, George and I were treated to about half a dozen free shows!

One of these was at the Palladium, which was only about fifty yards from where I worked. It starred Eddie Fisher, who sang at the start of a variety show. This was about 1950 and Mr Fisher looked about twenty-five. We got to the performance late and – very self-consciously – made our way to our seats at the end of the front row, by the aisle.

Everyone else had arrived by this time so, causing the greatest of embarrassment for us, he stopped singing and said, "Oh, I'll start again then," before doing just that!

One very famous man, the comedy actor George Robey, gave me a signed photograph of himself. It showed him wearing his usual comical bowler hat and pulling a funny face, just as Charlie Chaplin would have done in *his* films. He must have been about fifty years of age by then.

Then Rhona once more

About 1950, I saw my sister, Rhona, for the last time. George and I were on a bus, while Rhona sat several rows ahead. She gave us a serious glance as she was getting off and made no friendly acknowledgement that she knew us as she did so. I only noticed her as she passed me.

Afterwards, George asked, "Who was that?"

"That was my sister, Rhona. She left us years ago with my dad."

She stepped out onto the pavement and walked away. I feel no sadness that I never saw my 'sister' Rhona again.

The new flat in Haringey

Around the same time, my family was offered a fourth-floor residence in a new block of council flats in Haringey. It was very modern, offering convenient, safe electric lighting; our own toilet and separate bathroom; and three proper bedrooms. The picturesque view of lines of large trees and open spaces in the distance made us feel as though we were in the country, and privileged to have been given a place in such an apparently upmarket part of London.

The decision

As my association with George became more serious, certain 'frictions' began to occur between him and my family. Arthur – having spent the later war years with my mother, giving her some much-needed support – seemed to be expecting me to make up for the lost time and remain in her household. I think that she feared me leaving home and losing the assistance and support that I could now offer her. Meanwhile, I was beginning to fear remaining at home and never having the possibility of getting away.

One day, opinions became intransigent and the disagreement, vitriolic. I stormed out of the flat and started to take a long walk – south, towards the Thames. I spent several minutes staring at the hypnotic, fast-flowing water before taking a step back, to make a lengthy and far more considered reappraisal of my situation. I realised that if George loved me, he would be the solution to my current troubles rather than the cause of them. With my newly found confidence and clarity of design, I turned around and made my way back to George's house, to let him prove himself... or give me up. For whatever I was going to discover, I lost all apprehension.

When I arrived so unexpectedly at his house, George asked me what I was doing there. I explained about the row over him that I had had with my mother and Arthur, and my long period of contemplation beside the Thames. He immediately took me inside.

He quickly came to terms with the sudden, earnest turn of events and, despite my family's strong disapproval, proposed. To alleviate my temporary problem with accommodation, George's brother Ted generously offered to let me stay with him and his wife in their house in nearby Lever Street.

Two weeks later, on a fine, sunny day in November 1952, George and I got married. The ceremony was held at the local registry office. The only witnesses were my sister, Nancy (the only member of my family to attend), accompanied by her new boyfriend, Bobby, who had recently moved to London from Wales, and George's parents.

It did not go unnoticed that I was marrying in the same year in which Queen Elizabeth had acceded to the throne. My husband and I felt in good company – to be starting our lives anew, so soon after such an important person had so unexpectedly also begun her new role in life.

However, although it was heartening to be able to claim such an association of circumstances, there the similarities ended, for George and I had no palatial home to which we could retire. We were directly going to have to search for our home. Nevertheless, for the moment, we relaxed. We indulged in a few hours of merrymaking with our new in-laws. We circulated and conversed with everyone as the new husband and wife. Our emotions were at their highest, our hearts at their lightest. We had time, yet, to think about the problems of tomorrow.

Married life begins

George's inauspicious and uncomfortable Spartan single-young-man's bedroom had to suffice for our marital sleeping arrangements until we were able to secure a small downstairs flat in nearby Harman Street. It had a kitchen, and a lounge that doubled as a bedroom by the expediency of having a sofa bed within it.

We eventually had our honeymoon – a couple of weeks in the summer, at Ramsgate. The weather stayed fine, as we had hoped, and we had a very enjoyable time. At one point, we were surprised when the actor Roger Moore made an unexpected appearance nearby, on a path beside the beach. He was appearing in a stage play in the town and, when we saw him, he was talking to a woman while a group of other people attentively stood around him.

We felt gratified that such a well-known person should have chosen the time to be at the resort when we were there as well! It was an *extra* pleasant little highlight that made the occasion even more memorable.

And more changes....

By 1955, George and I kept changing the places where we lived. As we were on better terms with my mother and Arthur, we moved in with them for a while before moving into various other places around London.

Within weeks, Nancy married Bobby but because we were not near them at the time, we unfortunately knew nothing about it and could not reciprocate the attendance at their wedding.

The living arrangements at our Highbury Corner flat – like so many previous places – were basic. The only way to get sufficient quantities of hot water for our bath, which was a small portable one, was to utilise our large, grey, floor-standing 'copper' pot. Previously, our laundry would have been washed in it, so we first had to rinse the inside of it and then fill it with bowls of cold water from the single tap in the sink. We then boiled the water and transferred it to the bath via its outlet hose. Using that method, it took at least fifteen minutes to produce an adequate amount in which to bathe.

As an alternative, I went to the public baths two or three times. They were about a mile and a half away, near Chappell Street, so I usually went by bus. George did not bother with it and continued bathing at home.

When I got there, I went to the women's section, paid the required amount, and I was then given a numbered ticket. If necessary, by paying some more money, I could have hired a towel (which was usually not wonderful quality) or bought a small bar of soap.

Holding my soap and towels, I then went upstairs and waited on one of the ten or so chairs in the hallway. There were plenty of other women and girls there, who were each awaiting their turn to have a bath. There were a similar number of bathrooms down the corridor; we each had to wait for one of the current occupants to finish their quick splash around before the next person in the queue would be allowed in, to commence her bath.

Bathers were allowed fifteen minutes in a bathroom, after which time they had to leave. The bathroom doors were only closed – not locked – so there was no possibility of someone who had not yet finished, preventing the attendant going in and removing her. However, I never heard of any 'slow' bathers having to be dragged out of a bath... *"Hang on a minute! I ain't done me feet yet!"*

The bath was quickly rinsed and then refilled by the attendant to a satisfactory temperature. I was then left alone, to undertake my ablutions. There was no time for relaxing, singing or daydreaming in the bath – it was a case of getting in, washing and getting out again. I washed franticly, knowing that I had to finish before the attendant would expect me to vacate the room, to allow the next person in.

If I failed to finish my bath before my time was up, well, that was just tough, as it was put. Then, my only recourse would have been to go downstairs, pay another entrance fee and start all over again; it was not possible to pay twice as much and then take twice as long.

I never knew anyone who had another fifteen-minute bath, though. No one wanted the inconvenience of queuing up again in order to get wet and dry for a second time. The fear of such aggravation was enough to ensure that all ablutions were carried out quickly and were subsequently accomplished by the end of the first visit.

It was not a comfortable experience. I felt that the establishment was too communal for what should have been a solitary occasion; it was a bit like queuing to use a public toilet.

After having my bath, I took a bus back home. Eventually, I preferred the bathing arrangements at home. Although there was laborious preparation involved, there was the benefit of more privacy and a lot less travelling!

...and then CHANGES

After a time, problems arose between George and me. He was gambling and losing quite a bit of money at the greyhound races, and the insecure circumstances of where we were living only aggravated matters.

We separated for a few days but with a little kiss and a cuddle, and forgiveness, we became a couple again and returned to our flat at Highbury Corner.

Janice is coming... JANICE IS COMING!
By the late 1950s I became pregnant. When my time of giving birth approached, I made my way to the nearby hospital. I was put into one of the beds in the maternity ward and reassured by the nurses that everything would be all right. They did not expect me to give birth immediately, so they tended to leave me alone.

Many hours passed and the night came. Then, worryingly, I began to get pains down below. My unborn child had not been told that it was not supposed to emerge for some time; now it appeared to be starting to work to its own timetable. I felt that something was going seriously wrong. I was not as certain as the nurses had been that everything was going to be all right and that my child's birth was not imminent. My concerns grew with every passing minute.

I called out for help but no one came, so I called out again. Still no one came. I could see a pattern emerging. As I looked around, I saw a complete absence of medical personnel. I realised that my earlier fears of giving birth alone had come true.

There were a few women in the other beds, who were mostly awaiting their turn to partake in the delights of childbirth. It was night-time and most of them seemed eager to try to sleep through my apparent forthcoming agony. Some others just held fearful, apprehensive expressions or stared at me with looks of despair that did little to allay my worries about the coming night. Some offered me their moral support, while others, I think, preferred me just to proceed with a little less noise. I expected proper medical intervention at my hour of need, rather than dread or a few words of encouragement from my fellow patients. All looked far from their peaks of physical fitness – half seemed ready to go into labour with the first careless sneeze... from anyone! I could hardly expect help from any of them.

What was I to do, I wondered. My unborn baby was

getting restless and so was everyone else. I decided that I was not going to suffer quietly. I tried calling out for a nurse one more time and someone else even joined in with me but it was still to no avail; my natural instincts had to take over. The time to procrastinate was ending.

I began doing the heavy breathing and screaming thing that all mothers-to-be get to do when they think that they are going to have a child. I prepared myself to follow nature's chosen direction and began pushing.

After a time, when things began to get a little easier, I took a few moments to relax and get my breath back. I looked down at my bed, which had earlier been so neatly made; now, it was quite a shambles.

Then, one of the nurses finally decided to come up to me. She went straight to the end of the bed. I was expecting to be told off for messing up all of her nice neat sheets, and if that was the only reason for which she had just come in, I thought, then I was going to have a thoroughly good moan at her. I was preparing all of the right words with which I was going to berate my absent 'carer'.

Then I saw some things moving at the end of the bed that had not been there only a few moments earlier. There were definitely two legs sticking up... and they were definitely not mine! They were far shorter, for a start, and they were wriggling around. They were certainly not the nurse's, either! She was standing by the end of the bed. She leant over, picked up something cute and pink that had been wobbling about on the bed-clothes, and then gently handed to me my own just-arrived, beautiful little baby.

As she did so, she proudly added, "There you are, Lilian. It's your new baby daughter," behaving as though she had actually had some kind of significant input in the output.

I could hardly believe my eyes. After all of the agony, my baby had suddenly come out without me noticing! I cradled her in my tired arms (my new baby, that is, not the nurse). I was cuddling the latest little piece of humanity – the child that had rushed to appear, so that its mother was not left quite so alone in this world, after all.

My new child, upon its unexpected entry into this world, received no slap on its back (either for health or punishment reasons...) *"What are you doin' out this time of night?!"*

It was, I hoped, a sign of good fortune ahead. Its umbilical cord was clamped and then snipped by the nurse, who immediately turned and pointed at the coming halo of light that was breaking through the curtain of darkness outside.

"Look at that," she said. "It's dawn now."

So it was, that around four o'clock in the morning my baby was born. In recognition of the fact that she had seemed so eager to present herself at such a beautiful beginning of a new day, we were to bestow upon her the middle name Dawn.

George came and saw the pair of us that evening. He took his new, soft, little bundle of joy in his strong arms, and cradled her. He spoke to her with expressive phrases of love and joy such as "Oochy, coochy, coo" and "Wibbly, wibbly, wibbly", while we both tickled her under the chin. She responded by blowing bubbles through the saliva that freely dribbled out of her partly opened mouth.

It was the proudest moment of our lives and now we were really starting to feel like a proper family. We took our time and then named our newest addition to it, Janice.

After about five or six days, I went back home with my new baby daughter, Janice. Before leaving, I complained to the hospital authorities about the medical intervention that was lacking when I had earlier needed it. I explained that it had forced me to undertake a do-it-yourself childbirth, but nothing worthwhile came of it (the complaint, that is, not the childbirth). All of the nurses and doctors just gave excuses for each other's absences.

My satisfaction, though, was that at least no serious complications materialised during the birth and it worked out all right in the end.

24

Departures, arrivals, new lessons, new moves

Laney buildings

AFTER TWO YEARS in our small accommodation, we acquired a Laney Buildings' flat, which was larger than our previous one. Unfortunately, it had no bathroom, so George and I had to utilise public baths once more, which were about half a mile away at Ironmonger Row. However, Janice's small size meant that she could be bathed indoors, in our portable tin bath.

Another arrival

A few years after Janice came into our lives, my other child – Stephen – was born. His entry into this world was far more conventional than his sister's – that is, he did not surprise everyone with an unexpected early-morning delivery. He arrived somewhat punctually and with a full head of red, curly hair (that is, his own head had lots of tight auburn curls upon it – he was not delivered with a 'supplementary' head full of hair!)... *"There you go, Lilian – your new baby boy. And here's your new, free, hairy head to go with him!"*

In recognition of his father, we gave him the middle name George. By now, Janice began her schooling, and I gave up work in order to look after her and Stephen full-time.

Porridge!

Janice's early education received a setback one day when I gave her porridge for the first time, for breakfast. The long time that she spent slowly consuming it, led to her being late for school.

Upon her arrival, the teacher asked, "Janice, why are you late?"

Janice approached the high inquisitor with an air of endearing supplication.

"Mum made me eat porridge," the child humbly explained.

Fortunately, Janice's 'porridge trauma' was accepted as a valid reason for turning up late, and she was forgiven.

George 'meets' the Queen

As a security attendant at Kenwood House, George was thrilled one day when Queen Elizabeth glanced at him as she viewed the artworks. He said that she looked quite attractive and, had they met a few years earlier, he might have married her instead... although I doubt that that could quite have happened, somehow.

The Guildhall and the day Prince Philip spoke

George also worked at London's prestigious Guildhall. As a security attendant once more, he issued and received very old – and valuable – books and documents. He proudly boasted that, while in the library, he maintained a proper academic ambience and ensured that there was no running around, silly noises or flicking of rubber bands at anyone by any of the academics; and no squabbles or fights ever broke out among the intelligentsia, perhaps over who owned the best pencil case!

One evening, Prince Philip arrived with another famous person for a series of speeches. When they were about to start, the more important attendants ushered George and all of the other less important attendants outside of the great hall and then the doors were firmly shut. However, intense curiosity persuaded each of them afterwards to spy through the door's small keyhole, to discover what was happening on the other side (George and his companions were trying to spy on Prince Philip and his acquaintance, not the other way around). Their efforts, though, were in vain.

A room of their own, a garden, a first day at school and family holidays too!

In 1966, we moved into a three-bedroom house in Tottenham. Now, each of our children had their own bedroom as well as access to a garden where they could go outside and play in safety. We were not particularly wealthy but George somehow always managed to find enough money to keep us contented. We had a holiday together every year, usually somewhere like Clacton, the Isle of Wight or Walton-on-the-Naze.

In 1968 – on his fifth birthday – Stephen started school. After his first day there, he was shocked to learn that his education had not yet finished and that, in fact, it would continue for over ten more years! He cried upon hearing the shocking revelation.

Janice and Stephen were getting on very well and always enjoyed playing together. Her brother remembers that, many times, Janice held him upside down and then swung him around for a while, either in one of the bedrooms – on top of a bed – or outside in the garden.

Nevertheless, even now, Stephen proudly says that despite all of that 'violent' inverted swinging around that Janice used to do to him, he 'never gave her the money!'

George's new job

George's next job was as a bus conductor. While he was learning to stand upright on the bus at the same time as he was collecting the fares and issuing tickets, fewer and fewer passengers were being elbowed or pushed by him. However, the number of those being injured increased sharply when the bus, upon which he was standing, actually began moving.

The prefab
By now, Nancy and Bobby had moved into a 'prefab' in Dalston. Prefabs – prefabricated buildings – were mass-produced temporary replacements for the many homes that were damaged or destroyed during the war. Made of cheap materials and meant to last for only about twenty years, prefabs were nevertheless smart and perfectly adequate for a young and growing family, which suited Nancy and Bobby, as they now had two children, Leon and Michelle.

Mother helps to motivate my children
When my mother came to see us, even though she only had her pension to live on, she always brought a little treat for us such as a cake, or – for the children – something like the educational magazines *Look and Learn* and *World of Wonder*. She was always pleased to hear how well Janice and Stephen were doing in school and they were always pleased to let her know.

Stephen starts at a new school... eventually
In the mid-1970s, we moved to Hertfordshire. Stephen, after having spent three months at a London comprehensive, now needed a new school to attend. After some disappointments, George eventually found a good one that had half a dozen vacancies – a comprehensive that had been a grammar school only a couple of years before. It had a uniform, better facilities than Stephen's previous one and a better curriculum. However, because they were just over three miles away, they wanted to reserve their vacancies for the local children.

George spent about half an hour trying to persuade the

deputy headmaster to relent and allow my boy to fill one of those vacancies. He was successful in his dogged efforts, and Stephen started at the establishment within days. My son immediately found the level of discipline and motivation of the teachers much better than at his previous school.

George and I were always to see that Stephen was to take full advantage of the establishment, and not waste the opportunity – the good start in life – that we had given him.

The milk, the biscuits and the field of fire

One day, the field that was adjacent to our house, which was situated at the edge of the estate, caught fire. It had been a particularly hot summer and the parched grass coincidentally caught alight when many of the bored local youths were on their school summer holidays.

One of the firemen attending the blaze told everyone in our row of houses to evacuate them. I instinctively grabbed a bottle of milk and a packet of biscuits and put them both in my handbag.

My son asked why I was taking them with me as we left the house and I just automatically replied, "For something to eat and drink, if we need them."

What I had done was not reasoned at that moment in time but was a copy of my mother's practice from the time of the air raids – when she usually took a bottle of milk to drink, and some biscuits to eat, in the shelter. I had subconsciously adopted the emergency drill and it had stayed dormant within me and unused for over thirty years, until another emergency had reactivated it. When one is in danger, it is surprising what deep memories and automatic life-saving practices return to the fore.

Stephen does well at school

Stephen did well at school. He received prizes for maths and art, and became one of only two pupils – out of about a hundred and fifty from his year – to pass all eight O levels. The other child who passed all eight was a girl called Jane – a nice friend of his who acquired the nickname 'Tarzan'.

If she is reading this and she recognises herself and remembers Stephen (which my son admits is probably quite unlikely), then he would like her to know that he hopes that she has done well in her life. In fact, if anyone with whom he went to school remembers him (fondly), such as Paul, then he wishes them well too.

He would also like to pass on his gratitude to his many teachers who helped him at school, especially Mr Healing and others of the English Language department who, he said, learned him how to rite more proper... Hmm...!

The return to London and work... of a sort
In the early 1980s, the whole family moved back to London. George was now working as a drawing office clerk in a printing room where copious amounts of ammonia were always being used. The atmosphere was so bad that the draughtsmen who entered his room could not exit quickly enough and they always made sure that the door was kept closed so that no one else in the office could breathe the fumes and become ill – except George, of course. Because the room was small and only contained a limited amount of oxygen, George opened his window (in all weathers) to allow the fresh air (with oxygen) in and the gas out but then he got cold during the winters.

His boss did not lack compassion, though. He considerately helped George to stay alive through the freezing winter months by thoughtfully furnishing him with a heater. In addition, to help distract George from any negative thoughts about hypothermia or asphyxiation – and his general physical deterioration – George was allowed to listen to Radio 2 via his personal headphones, which was something that the draughtsmen were not allowed to do because they were not being slowly killed.

By 1987, though, George went to see his doctor about his working environment (George's environment, not the doctor's), who recommended that he should give up the terrible job for the sake of his own health (the doctor recommended that George should give up *his* terrible job, not the other way around), which George did.

Stephen aims higher

Stephen stayed at school for two more years, to do A levels, and then went out to work. After failing to make any significant progress within the organisations in which he worked, which included a depressing government department (its purpose was not to function that way – it just did), he decided to return to full-time education as a mature student (a title that, he acknowledged, referred only to his physical age). Unfortunately, no one from either my family or George's had ever entered further education, so, struggling for careers advice as to which establishment he should choose, he made the rather radical decision of returning to his old school and speaking to his former mathematics teacher, Mr Charlton.

"Well, which one do you want to go to?" Mr Charlton simply asked Stephen.

Mr Charlton now helped Stephen one last time, encouraging (or forcing) him to be more self-deterministic. Stephen dutifully picked the one to which he would commit himself for three years.

My son then left his teacher and his school behind and, a few months later, went to that chosen university. He was happy, and also very proud, to know that he had given something to the school, something of his which would remain long after his presence would be forgotten – his name. It would be added to others on a shield that would hang high up in the school hall, acknowledging those pupils who went onto further education in 1987. A new shield is created each year, for that year's new undergraduates.

Although his name, sadly, did not sit with the names of those who had gone onto further education in 1982 – those with whom he had spent seven (long) years of schooling – it is written in glorious brilliant gold with the names of other students who were now climbing higher on the ladder of success. All of the shields throughout the years remain as an admirable inspiration to others: from the encouraging teacher, to the prospective undergraduate, to the newly arrived and inquisitive young pupil.

Back to work

About the same time that Stephen was preparing to go to university, Janice's German boss died of a heart attack. She had been working for him as his personal assistant. He was a nice man who had first come to this country as a pilot in the Luftwaffe when he was trying to blow it to bits.

After the war, he stayed in Britain and started a central heating company. He worked hard and built his business up from virtually nothing until it was eventually valued at around a million pounds. Then, a week before he was due to retire, he tragically dropped dead!

In the meantime, after having just given up his previous job on health grounds, George was pleased to find work immediately, about a mile away. Unfortunately, his duties involved him having to lift heavy car springs all day. He was warned that if he accidentally dropped any, his feet could be crushed or even partly cut off (merely a consequence of the spring hitting them, not a threat of punishment). George gave up the disquieting work after a couple of weeks.

When the Queen Mother saw Stephen

One day, when Stephen was just outside his university's

computer room, he most unexpectedly noticed the Queen Mother standing the other side of the glass-panelled doors at the end of the corridor! She was the patron of the university and, as part of her office, she was going on a walkabout around the grounds with several smartly dressed people.

Stephen stood with a couple of other students and watched as the Queen Mother, at the same time as she was speaking to one of the officials, slowly turned and looked sideways at Stephen for several seconds. Without changing her expression, she slowly turned her head forwards again, to continue her conversation.

"It was almost as though she couldn't quite make me out," Stephen explained, slightly with his tongue in his cheek.

After another minute or so, the royal visitor and her entourage carried on with their leisurely walk.

Janice flies the nest and Stephen is presented to the princess

Towards the end of the 1980s, we all moved to be near to Stephen, to alleviate his protracted accommodation problems, which included sleep deprivation. Now he was able to concentrate properly on his studies.

Janice met her future husband, Simon, at this time. They married soon after and immediately moved into their new home, which was about ten miles away.

After three years' hard work, Stephen finally achieved an honours degree in Computer Science. George, Stephen and I then moved back to Hertfordshire.

Later that year, George and I proudly attended the presentation of our son to Princess Anne at the Royal Albert Hall. George and I were allocated seats at the front of the top balcony, which were not entirely suitable for people with a fear of heights – which included me, unfortunately.

Beneath the balconies sat the students, and in front of

them – in the centre of the hall – were seated the rest of the parents. Princess Anne was sitting in the middle of the stage. Apart from one girl who had dressed casually, every other graduate was properly dressed in a black gown, mortar-board and specific hood that identified the faculty in which he or she had excelled.

After a few introductory speeches by the dignitaries, including Princess Anne, each group of the one thousand or so graduates – having previously been seated according to their particular faculty – was called and lined up at the side of the stage.

My son stood apprehensively when it was his turn. He had a sense of pride and satisfaction, knowing that he had surpassed the expectations of so many people and had achieved a degree that was comparable to that of so many other students who had come from far more privileged backgrounds.

When his name was called, Stephen did as others had done before him and others would do afterwards. He went up to Princess Anne – who was seated a few feet in front of him on a ceremonial chair – bowed to her and then walked off the other end of the stage. Finally, about six doctors and professors were called to the princess.

George, Stephen and I enjoyed ourselves greatly during the three hours that we spent at the Royal Albert Hall. It was a grand occasion, which acknowledged so many personal achievements. We would never forget that most memorable of days.

25

An 'ending'

George
IN THE MID-1990S, George retired. Almost immediately, he confronted a new problem – one that none of us has ever experienced. It was cancer. However, after a period of chemotherapy, he has thankfully been given the all-clear.

Janice
My daughter has been a secretary/personal assistant in several prestigious organisations. In her spare time, she enjoys writing and doing amateur dramatics. Her husband has constantly been a good provider.

They have one child, a boy, who has inclinations towards technology and a great love of the outdoor life. All of their parental love will be laid upon him.

Janice keeps a happy and contented family.

Stephen
My son currently spends much of his time helping me to complete this book. He has not yet married but one day he hopes to meet a woman who can abide his weird sense of humour... before he dies. He constantly worries, though, that any prospective future wife might be put off by his dreadful incessant snoring (which sounds even worse when he actually falls asleep).

Arthur

Arthur became romantic for a while when he spent a few months going out with a French woman. He could speak no French, and she, virtually no English. To him, he had found the perfect woman. The relationship did not last long.

Arthur likes to make people think that he is a wealthy retired managing director of a multinational corporation. To keep up the pretence, he often fearlessly spends huge sums of money in pubs and betting shops. Sometimes, he even casually re-bets winnings of hundreds of pounds. Typically, he loses the bets and then has to try to survive the rest of the week until his next pension payment arrives.

About fifteen years ago, he was mugged for not much money by a couple of young men. Afterwards, he needed some hospital treatment for a bruised eye. Perhaps he had been acting wealthy too convincingly, although, of course, that does not excuse the crime. His attackers were never found.

The last time that I heard about Arthur's rather esoteric, hermit-like existence, he was living somewhere in north London.

Nancy

Nancy's daughter, Michelle, is still living with her. Her son Leon is married with two children.

Joan

My sister Joan married an American soldier, who whisked her off to America. After they had one child – Carol – he unfortunately divorced her.

Carol became quite a 'free spirit' who found great opportunities to express herself in the 'land of the free'. She has more recently begun raising two children of her own, and become the mature, sensible and loving mother whom we all knew she would turn out to be.

John
John married Jennie in a large church wedding. After giving her two children to bring up, he divorced her and is now living with another woman.

Aunts and uncles
It is unfortunate that I did not see more of my Aunt Eleanor and her husband Henry, and Freda and her husband, for I found them very warm and kind people, and they are not around anymore.

Mother
My mother only recently divorced my father, after he had repeatedly asked her to do so. For many years, he had been living with another woman. Ironically, he died soon afterwards and all of his possessions were left to his new wife!

My mother continued her lifelong passion for her 'daily dose of medicine' – her can of beer. Arthur – who had lived with, and cared for, his mother almost constantly – was always able to ensure that she had a ready supply of it.

As the years passed, my mother's physical ailments increased but she was always uncomplaining. Her deeply held religious beliefs probably helped to sustain her through life's less pleasant times.

Travelling from Kent to Haringey most weekends, Nancy undertook the essential care routines of my mother, such as the washing and styling of her hair.

Unfortunately, Arthur once walked out and left his mother for a week while she was not in the best of health. Then, on a pretext, other members of the family took her out and promptly deposited her – against her wishes – in a care home. They then returned to her flat without her permission and took from it numerous essential household items such as blankets, sheets and even the kettle!

After several months, Arthur collected my mother from the care home and returned her to her flat, where *he* looked after her for the last year of her life. Unfortunately, he had first to replace many of the household items that had been taken.

Last year, my mother was in hospital with a bout of pneumonia. There, the determined lady made no secret of her wish to go home again. Her vocal demands were only finally hushed by a dosage of hospital-administered sedatives. Having survived almost the entire twentieth century and nearly making it to a hundred, she quickly succumbed to the medication. Her loving son Arthur was with her in the ward as she was leaving us.

There was little of value left in her flat when she died but whatever there was, it went to Arthur. As to what happened to the dozen sovereigns that my mother once told me were hidden away for an emergency, I shall probably never know. I do not know whether they even really existed!

What Arthur inherited did not remain with him for long. Within a matter of weeks, he just walked out of the flat again. He left everything behind and never returned.

What I was left with, at the end of my mother's life, was the memory of her always being caring towards my family and generous to my children. My mother – as a mother should – left me with something more precious, enduring and far more valuable than gold.

... and me...

As for me, in my retirement I enjoy pottering about in the garden and watching the television, although I tend to do the latter more than ever now, as I am finding it increasingly difficult to do physical things like moving around. Consequently, George is spending his retirement doing more and more of the housework.

When I think of this book, which is so nearly finished, and

the story of my life's journey that shall be in it, I cannot help being moved at how so much of my life – and my family's – was determined by so many (often apparently trivial) events that were out of our control. If there had been no war, I would not have gone to Tenby and met the Morgans. If I had been given a typewriter in my first job in London, I would not have left the organisation, to work at Nottidges; and then I would never have met George, and had Janice and Stephen. If I had not had the academic inspiration from the Morgans, there might not have been the encouragement of my son to go to university. We might not have moved to be near him and then Janice would not have met her husband. Her son would never have been born.

How differently things might have worked out.

A debt of gratitude
I should like to acknowledge a debt of gratitude to the families with whom I stayed during the war, in particular the Morgans. Their act of exceptional altruism – due in part to their Quaker beliefs, facilitated by our churches and performed at a time of dire national emergency – might have saved many children's lives, including mine.

Mr Morgan was like a surrogate father to me. He taught me how to get the most from an education system that was expected to function normally even under particularly difficult wartime restrictions. However, he failed in his attempt to get me to stay in Wales in order to develop my singing voice.

The good Mr and Mrs Morgan were inspirational survivors who directed their children into respectable careers: Gly went to a suitably prestigious college in London to take exams in order to become a teacher. Gly, Alun, Idris and Ray were left a grand hotel to live in and run. In an absolute contrast, my father just left his children.

If there has been any historical debt of gratitude still to be paid, then I hope that it has been done in this book – albeit indirectly and rather belatedly.

The legacy of war
Before the war, the charitable organisation The Salvation Army helped people who were suffering destitution and hunger. My mother and her family were some of those who unfortunately became indebted to it during a period of particular personal misfortune.

I have always remembered The Salvation Army's acts of kindness – their supply of food that staved off the hunger – and, in later years, I have always tried to repay that debt by putting money in their tins whenever their charity workers have been collecting on the streets.

People like my mother dreamed of better times. What they were given instead was the Second World War! Millions died in it. Many were innocent civilians who were dispatched in the most terrible of circumstances. 'Lucky' survivors were often left scarred, both physically and emotionally.

Millions of children were evacuated from the cities for their own protection. Many suffered, especially those who were never to return home – their war would be never-ending.

At the end of hostilities, a spirit of humanity spread to the masses of this country, who wanted a 'new world' for themselves as a reward for their efforts in helping to bring about such a peace. They wanted compensation for their suffering and the many sacrifices that they and their families had endured.

The outlook for many people's lives began to look promising when they actually started to receive what they had so long hoped for. The new institutions of a proper welfare state and a free National Health Service arrived. The poor could now be given respite; and the sick, who could not previously afford the care, could now be cured or freed from pain.

Cheap council housing replaced millions of damaged or destroyed homes, many of which had been squalid; for the first time, people with limited incomes were allowed to bring up their families in decent accommodation – they would no longer fear the wrath of a greedy private landlord.

It finally appeared that the pre-war levels of misery that so many people once knew were now to be consigned permanently to the more unpleasant pages of history.

Letting go

Here ends my tale of the life of a London girl. Like the RAF's motto, *Per ardua ad astra* – Through adversity to the stars (which is Stephen's favourite phrase) – it is of inspiration and the will to succeed against the odds. It is of closed windows of opportunity that are opened by faith, perseverance and a greater understanding, and knowledge, of life.

It is a document of the spirit, the mind and the heart. It is completed by loyalty, enduring love and dedication to, and from, those around me. It is such a collection of thoughts, written down and left behind.

26

Where the spirit takes us

An extra chapter, by Stephen White

The 'jigsaw'

NOW THAT ALL – or virtually all – of the book has been read, I shall provide some more information about the story's construction, starting with my mother's description of her evacuation with Doris to a place that was like a farm. There, pigs were kept – and killed – for food. It was an environment that my mother did not like. She also spoke of the adoption of Doris by the farming family, and described it as the 'taking away' of her sister, an event for which she blamed the war. In her later years, although she was very curious as to what had happened to her sister, she was worried that any reunion with her would be a cause of great emotional upset.

Relatives also became a useful source of information for this book. For instance, I contacted Lilian's brother Arthur, and gained a little (I emphasise the word 'little') information of their family history from him. Arthur remembered being evacuated to the same place that Doris went – the farm, which was in Lincolnshire or Lancashire – but he could not remember being there with my mother. That coincided somewhat with my mother's account, except that she could not remember being on the farm with Arthur! However, that did not explain how Arthur and my mother were both at the farm, at the same time, with Doris!

Arthur remembered chasing the farm animals, and that

he did not like some of them (perhaps they also did not like him – especially if they suspected they were about to be killed!). He eventually left the farm and was evacuated to other places.

Because of the short period of time that he was at the farm, possibly with Lilian, and because of the ambiguities to do with geographical locations, I decided that it was prudent to write Arthur out of the farm aspect of the story. I concentrated instead on the elements of the evacuation that had substantial accuracy. I noted, however, that there was an apparent early emotional distance between Arthur and my mother, which I found useful when defining their characters.

Lilian had told George (my father) a lot about her early life. They lived near each other in the 1930s (although they did not know each other then) and their social circumstances were similar, so a great deal could be surmised about Lilian's young life, after a bit of careful thought.

Elsie – George's sister – gave a lot more personal information about the period leading up to the war. She also explained some of the work of the local committees that helped to organise the evacuations.

In addition, the areas to which Lilian was evacuated can still be seen, and with a general understanding of wartime necessities – such as barbed wire emplacements and always being on the lookout for spies – her missing wartime environments slowly began to take shape in the construction of the early drafts.

Lilian left clear descriptions of the Welsh caves and mines that she visited, and so many other things that still exist, that it became increasingly clear that a re-examination and expansion of her story was possible. Knowing her character at different times, I was able to begin composing many of the missing segments.

The project began to appear like a kind of historical

literary jigsaw puzzle that could lend itself to completion in the same way that the conventional board game could. The known facts were placed first within the book. Incomplete facts were the next to be placed; they were put in the most likely vacant segments but they were not allowed to contradict what was already known and they were subject to later changes. Assumptions – likely scenarios – filled in the major blanks. Where there were minor opportunities for a little light relief, I indulged my obscure sense of humour – one that was not too dissimilar to my mother's, so I did not feel that it was particularly inappropriate to do so. Thus, in time, the complete story of my mother's life began to take shape.

An example of such a method of composition is where I created a potentially fictitious scenario – such as my mother's feeding of the farm animals. Although I lacked many of the specific details, I tried to depict the events and any relationships at that point as realistically as possible.

Sometimes, I have had more information to utilise, such as the episode where Lilian had her mouth washed out with soap and water. It really happened to her but whether it actually occurred at school or when she was with the Morgans (Miss Dickinson certainly threatened the punishment), I cannot now say. However, I remembered what she had said about it a few years ago and wrote to convey those emotions and the facts that I knew.

I did the same where other events definitely occurred but where the details of them are unavailable. Such an example was when my mother parted from Doris. She was always to be troubled when remembering the sister left behind at the farm. I assumed that the experience of parting must have been very traumatic for them both and I hope that I have justifiably depicted it as such.

More information was taken from Lilian's many accounts of her family's pre-war relationships, and what she did not put down on paper she said to her family on other occasions and that is what I have used and written about.

Details of Lilian's early evacuation to the farm were sketchy, and therefore much of that period has been assumed. However, recently discovered notes have since described it as being located in Spalding. To avoid undesirably misrepresenting specific environments such as the local school, I only referred to her as living near to that town – not in it. The 'farming family' were reasonably well off and consisted of a husband – who was a *newsagent* – his wife, and two grown-up sons who were in their early twenties (one of whom looked like the actor Tyrone Power). What I described earlier as being a farm, was actually less 'glamorous'; in fact, it was a house with a very long back garden that had a river at the end of it. However, it was because of the quantity and variety of animals that were kept in the garden – and slaughtered there – that my mother always talked about it as though it was a farm. She hated the killing of the animals and found the butchering of the pigs particularly distressing. What she witnessed eventually drove her to leave the place and return to London.

Those recently discovered notes have also given a few more details about the second evacuation. My mother and her mother did not have a prior arrangement to go to the mansion but, instead, went to a hall in order to be chosen by the 'slave market' method. After being picked by a woman, they were escorted not to a mansion but to a castle! I remembered that my mother said that the furnishings were sparse and that they only had one room in which to live. However, they were not even fortunate enough to be given the luxury of mattresses on which to lie: in preparation for their arrival, just a few blankets had been arrayed on the bare wooden floorboards. The room that was intended to be theirs for the duration of the war was, otherwise, empty.

The story of Lilian's time with the Morgans contains a

large proportion of her original narrative and consequently describes events almost entirely as they really happened. She did fall off her bike as she went down a very steep hill, and was then almost run over by a lorry – all of which resulted in her being very seriously injured. She did almost drown. She did have swimming lessons and later saved her sister from drowning. She *was* cut off by the tide and then had to climb a near-vertical cliff in order to escape her predicament. She did meet the Italian POWs. She definitely or almost certainly visited the kinds of places that I described. The only liberties that I have taken are that I added some of the dialogue and drama to the day trips that she undertook because I am sure that she would have said and done similar things.

Post-war, the book contains the more personal experiences of both my father and me. I hope that they have given a more complete picture of my mother's life, being not only a kind of 'what happened next' but also a sort of 'what happened eventually'! For much of that part of the narrative, my father's help has been invaluable. His knowledge of the part of London where he used to live and work has seemed virtually limitless.

Another life-saver?

One final point that I would like to add, concerns my mother's accident with the lorry during the war years – when she could have been killed, had the driver not attended to his vehicle's brakes that same day. It inspired me to check my apparently roadworthy vehicle's brakes, whereupon I discovered that they had virtually no braking material left! I replaced them at the earliest opportunity.

I find it somewhat ironical that my life – and my father's life, if he had been travelling with me – could indirectly have been saved by the foresight of someone whose similar actions some sixty-odd years earlier had saved my mother's life!

And what of Doris?

Lilian often wondered what became of her sister. When her mother was visiting us a few years ago, Lilian tried to start a conversation about Doris, in the hope of eliciting some information.

"I wonder what happened to Doris," she said.

Her mother became serious and curtly responded, "I don't want to talk about it!"

I do not think that her mother was angry with anyone. It just seemed that the question had brought to mind the daughter who had never returned, and she was upset by it.

I found it moving that my mother still remembered Doris fondly, even into her twilight years. It was around such a relationship of sisterly love and devotion, that I constructed some of my early parts of the narrative. It also inspired me, a while ago, to make some preliminary attempts at trying to discover what actually did happen to Doris – to make the story more complete, so to speak – but I found the process daunting.

I immediately resolved to undertake any investigative work upon the completion of this book. It would then be for personal reasons instead of literary ones and I could spend more time on the lengthy detective work that I now realised would be involved. I was also aware that many decades had passed since she was last seen and that any efforts might all be for nothing, so I thought that it was best to complete one marathon job first before starting the next – possibly futile – one!

Then something most unexpected happened. In fact, something incredibly unexpected happened. It was the last day of July 2007. My father was downstairs in the lounge, watching the television as usual and I was upstairs in my room, typing. Suddenly, I heard the doorbell ring and wondered who was calling.

I stopped my work and went to the top of the stairs,

where I saw my father slowly going to the front door. He opened it a little. There was no one in the immediate vicinity. For a minute or so, he stood perplexed. Then a woman of somewhat advanced years apprehensively approached the house and stood on the doorstep.

"Yes?" my father asked.

The woman seemed a little nervous and just as unsure of herself and to whom she was speaking, as my father was. When no one had appeared to be coming to the door, she asked our neighbours nearby if they knew of any local people with our names. They directed her back to my father – who was now standing by the open street door – saying that he was the person she was after. I listened to this strangest of conversations from the top of the stairs.

"I was looking for a Lilian Smith... or a George White," she nervously uttered.

"I'm sorry but she passed away a few years ago. She was my wife," my father explained. "Who are you?"

"Oh," she said, apprehensively. "Oh... I'm Doris."

And so, after over 67 years (and what turned out to be two years of very laborious detective work by her son), Doris had finally restored contact with her blood relations.

"Come in. Come in," my father urged. She entered quite gingerly.

I ran down the stairs to meet the woman who I thought had been lost by her family decades ago. Moments before, she had been an enigmatic character from an incomplete book. Now, I stood in her presence as though she had just miraculously stepped out of it.

Her appearance was such that my father immediately thought that she resembled Lilian. Meanwhile, I thought that she looked more like a younger version of her mother.

"Do you know who this is?" my father asked me. I stood transfixed, half-smiling and incredulous. "This is your Aunt Doris!"

"No," I said, as though disbelieving my own eyes and ears.

Doris stood in the passage, unsure of how she would be received.

"Come inside," my father said, enthusiastically inviting her into the lounge.

"I've got my son outside in the car... with his children," she said.

"Well bring them in as well," I said, and so she did. She went back outside and returned a couple of minutes later with an entourage consisting of her son – who introduced himself as Peter – and his three boys, who were all about eight years of age.

The hellos that filled the air and the polite shaking of hands all seemed inadequate for such a momentous occasion; however, anything else more emotional would peculiarly – I felt – have been showing undue familiarity and would have been disrespectful. After all, we were all strangers who had never met before and yet, ironically, some of us had known of the others for all of our lives. What a truly strange moment in time we were all living.

Everyone entered the lounge, whence Doris began briefing my father and me as to how her life in Lincolnshire had turned out. She was evacuated with Arthur and Lilian to a house in Spalding, Lincolnshire, at the outbreak of war. The adults at the house kept chickens and pigs, which they killed when food requirements dictated. Along the back of the house, which is still standing, is a dyke.

The original allocation of a billet for Doris, Lilian and Arthur was not through the 'slave market' process – they were merely taken directly to the house. At this point, it is noteworthy that Doris remembered – even though she was only three years old at the time – that Lilian was present. When I had earlier sought information from Arthur about that period, he said that there was a sister with him, other than Doris, but that he could not remember her name. He is about five years older than Doris is and so, presumably, would have been more able to remember that my mother was with them.

My mother, interestingly, might also have been 'forgetful' about those with whom she was evacuated: she only spoke of an evacuation to a farm with Doris. She never mentioned Arthur, who – she said – was usually busy 'doing his own thing'.

As I have progressed with this book, I have found it increasingly easy to understand the problems – alluded to in previous chapters – that my mother had when she was younger, in relating to Arthur. It seems that from at least as early as 1939 until some time after she got married, both she and Arthur appeared to have been individuals with little in common.

When Doris arrived at her billet, it was realised that her original Christian name – which was not Doris – coincided with that of the woman to whom one of the householders' sons was engaged. In order to avoid confusion, the name Doris was chosen for my aunt. She was not unhappy with being allocated the new name and she retains it to this day.

(For the purposes of maintaining the anonymity of most of the people mentioned in this book, most of their actual names – including Doris' – are not the ones quoted in the text.)

After Arthur had temporarily run away from the house several times, someone went to it and took him back home. Doris last saw Lilian in late 1939, which was when Lilian returned home to London (where she remained until her next evacuation). Doris was adopted in October 1939. Now, only Doris and one other 'guest' (Mr Mares) were billeted in the 'farming' family house.

Doris then spoke briefly of her adoptive parents – of how they spent most of the next two decades dutifully bringing her up and how they only failed in one respect: they never loved her. My aunt suddenly punctuated her story of abandonment with silence and an expression of utter sadness. She tried to keep a stoical composure but it clearly hurt her, even now, to recall that lengthy poignant period of her life.

My father and I were so sorry to hear of such a tragic outcome of her evacuation; we *also* felt hurt. We had great pity for the lady and we expressed our sympathy to her – that she should have suffered so throughout her vulnerable formative years – but it was hard, perhaps impossible, to find the right words to say at such an occasion.

Doris asked me why it was that Arthur and Lilian went home, whereas she remained behind and was subsequently adopted. I explained that it was a wartime necessity that her mother allowed her to be adopted by a couple who apparently liked her so much that they wanted to keep her! I pointed out that if she had returned home while the war was still going on – particularly if she had gone back to London at a time of increasing fears of a German invasion – then she would probably still have been sent away again, albeit only for a temporary period. There was, of course, the possibility that the adults at any new billet would also have tried to adopt her. If, however, she had returned and stayed in London, she might even have been killed by the V-1 that later fell on her mother's house!

I told Doris that she and her many siblings were usually cared for by their mother alone, for their father was seldom seen in the house, and when Doris was allowed to be adopted, her mother was probably only doing what she thought was best. If Doris wanted to blame someone or something for her perceived abandonment, I said, then she should probably just blame the war. My aunt soon continued with the telling of her story.

When she got older, she went out to work. She spent seven years in a hotel – making beds and tidying the rooms for the guests – and was eventually responsible for laying the tables in the restaurant, just as her sister, Lilian, had done in her hotel. She then found work in a hospital – just as her mother had done! However, Doris' responsibilities were not the same as her mother's, as she fed the patients and looked after their general welfare.

When Doris was twenty-one, she had an operation to correct her badly aligned left eye. She may have had another operation before that but she cannot now remember. The result of the treatment was good and was particularly effective for about fifteen years.

She had another operation when she was about thirty or forty. Unfortunately, that had no effect, although looking into the beaming face of Doris now, one would never suspect that she had ever had any problems with her eyesight.

After working in the hospital for twenty-eight years, Doris retired to live – as she put it – 'the life of pleasure!'

Fate dealt Doris a kind and sturdy hand when it came to romance. Her choice of husband was a Polish gentleman who had suffered as a teenager when his homeland was defeated by the Nazi-Soviet aggressors.

Originally, he had been within the Nazi-occupied section, where he was soon given the starkest of choices: to undertake compulsory service for the German Reich or be *shot;* he chose self-preservation. However, he eventually managed to escape from his accursed situation. After making his way to Scotland, he grasped at the opportunity to take revenge on his erstwhile masters, and joined the Polish Parachute Brigade.

Fate was discerning when it spared him the disaster of Operation Market Garden – the ill-conceived parachute drop at Arnhem from which the understatement 'I think that we may have gone a bridge too far' was derived. Many of the gentleman's colleagues were part of the first wave and were killed or captured soon after being dropped into

Holland. He was due to be dropped as part of the second wave but that was cancelled when it was realised just how pointless it was to continue the doomed offensive. If he had gone into the battle, Doris' children – the cousins whom I am now getting to know – might never have been born, for he might not have survived and been around to father them.

Many years later, to commemorate the anniversary of the operation, he and all of the other Polish paratrooper veterans attended several grand parades in Holland. He often felt a little aggrieved, though, by the way that those marching at the front – those who were dropped at Arnhem, and survived – seemed to carry themselves.

However, all were worthy of praise from the people of Holland. All had been hardy, bold individuals who were willing and able to risk their lives in the dangerous cause of freedom; all were prepared to face the very real possibility of death in order to achieve the noble aim.

My uncle was clearly a very brave character indeed and I have nothing but the highest admiration for him, even just in recognition of his preparedness for the Arnhem adventure.

He died in 1996.

Doris has maintained contact with her husband's family – his brothers and sisters who live in Poland. She still sends them Christmas cards, and her family even visited them a couple of times. Although her husband's family was considered as living behind the Iron Curtain, they were never 'trapped' but were comfortable where they were and had no wish to emigrate.

She also happily remains in communication with her adoptive family. One of her adoptive parents' children is still alive; *his* children – and his late brother's – refer to her as their Auntie Doris.

When Peter was doing his detective work – examining various birth certificates while trying to trace us – he made a discovery concerning his mother that was rather unexpected: she had been celebrating her birthday for the past sixty-seven years on the wrong day! As she was so young when she was originally evacuated, she could not remember her correct birthday and no one had ensured that the day that she assumed was correct, was in fact so. Doris is now delighted by having been possessed of two different birthdays and now feels a certain sense of affinity with the Queen, a lady who has also been celebrating two birthdays each year: her real one and a pretend one!

When the conversation returned to the serious circumstances of my mother's death, Doris said that she had known about it for a while, having found out about the fate of her sister during the search for us. When she had been standing on our doorstep, saying that she was looking for a Lilian Smith, she knew that she would not meet my mother; she only mentioned Lilian's name as a way of introducing herself and explaining her presence.

Months earlier, she had questioned whether it was appropriate to continue looking for Lilian's family, knowing that her sister had died. Her son, however, seeking a clarification to part of his identity – his other family roots – was determined to continue and succeed with the investigative struggle.

Doris declared – on the very same day that she met us – that she wanted to get some flowers and place them upon her sister's grave. Such thoughtfulness and the fact that Lilian was the first person in her family whom Doris had tried to contact, has confirmed my belief that the ties between these two women, when they were young girls, was very close indeed.

The commendable various efforts that Doris and her son undertook for two years in order to trace Lilian's family, have moved my family and me very much. Their sense of belonging, which has lasted a lifetime and has subsequently been passed from the mother to her son, has been both admirable and surprising.

Before leaving us at the end of that first meeting, I was given the wonderful news that Doris has a daughter, Anthea, with three boys of her own. I have therefore not discovered one new cousin, but two! Likewise, my father now has several new relations – a new nephew and a new niece, to go with his new sister-in-law!

It then became the turn of my father and me to inform our visitors of their new relations! We gave Doris and her son the details of all of the other members of their family. Unsurprisingly, they did not even know many of them existed! Doris could now contact those who were still living, at her leisure.

Within a short time, Doris telephoned Janice. My sister was soon asked what she thought the reasons were that Doris was left behind at the 'farm' and was subsequently adopted. Doris suggested that it was perhaps because she was somehow deemed less than perfect, whereas Lilian, with her 'nice curly, blonde hair', was taken back by her mother.

Janice could offer no insight into what she thought the circumstances were that surrounded the adoption. She could only proffer a silent pause in the conversation. Afterwards, Janice telephoned me and we both agreed that it was very sad to think that our dear Aunt Doris has been harbouring such undeserved negative thoughts about herself for so long.

A few days after meeting us, Doris went to the Post Office to collect, from my father and me, a kind of 'welcome home' present – a little silver horseshoe on a necklace. It was reminiscent of the one that my mother had when she was in Wales, before *she* made her way home to her family.

It was also the eleventh anniversary of the death of Doris' husband, so she went into the florists to buy some flowers to put on his grave. As she was deciding which ones to buy, someone stole her purse, containing £160! Fortunately, her son was able to get some money to her, so she managed to survive the experience without too much inconvenience or trauma. It is very sad, though, that after all that my gentle Aunt Doris has been through in her complicated life – and especially when things appeared to be looking so positive for her – life still had something so base to put in the poor lady's way.

It's all getting very exciting!

Recently, Doris spoke for the first time to her sister, Joan, who is living in America. Joan is coming to England soon, when the pair of sisters will finally meet each other face to face.

"It's all getting very exciting!" Doris said to me on the phone, when she was talking about all of the members of her family whom she is now getting to see and find out about.

A few weeks later...

A few weeks later, Doris took her children with her to meet her remaining brothers and sister – Arthur, John and Joan – and her niece, Michelle, at a venue in north London. The occasion lasted a couple of hours. The somewhat shy Doris sat back, listening and learning of how the past sixty-seven years had treated her 'other' family. They, in turn, discovered how Doris' family life had taken a different journey but had, nevertheless, been at least as successful as theirs. Arthur did a lot of the talking; he had his moment of being the centre of attention, and seemed to revel in it.

Later, Arthur telephoned us. He usually does so every few weeks. I expected that he was going to talk about his meeting with Doris but when I asked him if anything had happened recently, he became very quiet and then spoke to my father about something completely unrelated and irrelevant.

To this day, he has never mentioned his meeting with Doris, despite the fact that he must be aware that we know that he has spoken to her; after all, we were the ones who gave his details to Doris! Sadly, he will probably always remain something of an enigma.

Doris said that the only sibling of hers whom she can really remember is Lilian. Perhaps that explains why, despite having just discovered that she is living only about a dozen miles away from Arthur, she has yet to visit her reclusive brother's hermitage.

In remembrance

In the summer of 2007, Doris and Peter came again to our house, this time accompanied by Anthea. They were all to meet Janice and her family for the first time. In preparation for the special event, Doris' hair had been specially dressed and she was particularly smartly attired. With Anthea's first visit, there was again a celebration in the house, at the meeting of more close relatives.

Doris' family were presented with a special silver-plated album that was filled with images they had never seen before of important periods in the lives of various family members. When Doris saw a photograph of Lilian appearing about nine years old, she quickly placed her hand upon it in a moment of emotion, as it so reminded her of a similar picture that had been taken of her, at about the same time.

Later, we all went to a nice restaurant, where Janice, Simon and their son Nicholas met Doris, Peter and Anthea for the first time. After the celebrations, my father and I – together with Doris' family – left the restaurant and travelled to the cemetery that was the last resting place of Doris' sister, mother and Aunt Eleanor. Lilian lies beside the secure company of her mother and her aunt. All three were buried in adjacent plots. Nancy, who had recently died of cancer, was cremated elsewhere. A marker stone of hers has been placed on her mother's grave.

As we stood before the large gravestones, Doris' children seemed relieved to have finally got as close as they could to their late close relatives but for Doris the occasion seemed to be one of greater poignancy – of a deeper meaning. She became quiet and stood deep in her thoughts. I asked her if she wanted to be left alone for a while beside the graves but she stoically declined and remained for several minutes with those who were standing with her.

Anthea remarked how unusually good the weather was staying beneath our particular part of the sky, almost as though the clouds were being kept apart just to help those who were there, to see more clearly. She looked around and then saw on the gravestone beside her, our grandmother's birthday: it was that very day, which we found a little moving.

My father spent about half an hour conveying once more to Doris the affection that my mother always had for her. If there was anything appropriate to add, I interjected with it; however, Doris and her family seemed adequately furnished with information supplied by my father. Although Lilian did not survive to meet her sister again, at least her husband and children have been blessed with the opportunity to pass on her loving sentiments towards her sister.

Those who stood with Doris that day, could see that she had an enduring love towards her family. She was stoic, with deep emotions; she stood as Lilian's equal.

Doris kissed her own hand and then placed it upon her sister's gravestone. She then did likewise with her mother's and aunt's gravestones. Anthea and Peter then copied their mother's tender example.

When the passage of time began dictating events, Doris and her children decided to part from the graveside but we still had time to visit the grave of George's mother, which was nearby. Doris' family followed us as we went to the plot. Once more, due respects were paid to the departed – even by those who had never even known the kind lady.

With that day's various 'missions' completed, we all left

the cemetery. My father and I led the way in our car back out of the city. Doris' family followed once more until they could, at last, find their own way home. It had been a long and moving day but one that had also – after the longest of waits – been most fulfilling.

Last Christmas, our first Christmas together

Just before Christmas 2007, Doris, Peter and Anthea returned to the cemetery to lay wreaths of different colours. Later, we all travelled to a nice restaurant, where, at one point, the conversation turned to that of the war years and Doris' evacuation.

I mentioned that Doris was privileged in that her hair was washed in Amari shampoo (by her mother, who also carefully styled it) whereas the hair of everyone else in her family, including Lilian's, was only ever washed in rainwater. As the conversation about Doris' pre-wartime, extra-special hair treatment continued, it was revealed that her hair was usually arranged into a little bun on the side of her head. Doris' children then put forward the interesting theory that, perhaps, that was merely to make Doris look more attractive to her future adoptive parents, solely in the hope that they would be more inclined to keep the cute little girl! No one took the idea too seriously and we all had a little laugh about it.

After a couple of hours, our families parted once more, although not before we all gave each other some unexpected Christmas presents!

Epilogue

Peter, Anthea, and Doris in particular, are people who have been kept apart from some of their blood relations for a very long time. Nevertheless, the many examples of kindness and thoughtfulness that they have unreservedly shown their kin over the past few months, are incomparable.

As I write the last few words of my mother's book – of her life – it gives me great pleasure that the story of Doris and her family can fill these final pages with distinction. I have such pride in my mother's family, that the sister to whom she was closest would have ended this story so.

About a million boys and girls were sent away for their own safety during the mass evacuation at the start of the war. Often, they left behind all that they knew and loved. Of those evacuees, a few thousand were adopted by their host families and never returned – or, at least, were never expected to!

Then, in 2007, one little girl did return. In the intervening years, however, she had become a mother of her own family and, thence, a grandmother as well. If she is not the only adopted evacuee who has managed to make her way back home again, then she must surely be one of only a few – one of the last 'casualties' of the Second World War, who is now a casualty no longer.

As I write of her now, it is with pleasure that I can do so in the present tense. She is no longer a distant character, lost in the first half of the twentieth century. Her name no longer conjures up only an indistinct thought – an ethereal echo of my mother's occasional sad reminiscences.

When Doris came into my life, it almost seemed that she had literally stepped out of the pages of this book. She has become a living aunt to me. She is a warm and friendly person who is justly living alongside her other remaining family members, now separated from most of them by only a hundred or so miles – just one tiny step in the sixty-seven years of a lost life.

Her well-educated family's success against the odds in their search for their other relations, is a fine example of an inspirational, indomitable spirit – a triumph of innately determined characters. That they tried to find us, was not entirely unexpected; that they were to succeed, was – in hindsight – inevitable. My family and I have just felt that it has been a great shame that those who knew Doris best – two of her sisters and her mother – never got to see her again. When Doris and her children were experiencing great moments in their lives, my family had no knowledge of it. When so many of my family were leaving us, they had no idea how much they were still thought of.

*

I would like to finish this literary enterprise by thanking a few people who helped me with so much of it. My father, George, helped me to fill in many of the gaps in my mother's story, especially the earliest and later ones. His sister Elsie also helped me with certain aspects of pre-war life and the evacuation. She spent many years in happy retirement on the southern coast of England but unfortunately died just before the publication of this book.

Doris, of course, has been essential for chapter twenty-six!

Thanks also go to my sister, Janice, for helping my mother to start this book, and for accommodating me in 2008 when I went on a couple of research trips for it, to a farm and Tenby. A little thank you goes to Arthur, as well, for the little information that he – not entirely lucidly – proffered.

A thank you goes as well to the current staff who are working in my mother's former school, Tenby County, which now functions as a local library. By most kindly giving me a historically detailed guided tour of all of its rooms, I was able to gain a better understanding and feel of my mother's final educational establishment.

Thanks are also due to health professional Diane Hewetson, who advised me about some of the modern medical procedures that surround childbirth. (In the text, not all of her advice was utilised – or even strictly adhered to!)

During the research for this book, while visiting some of the original locations, like Tenby, I inevitably also came close to some of the people described here-in. If, through the most innocent of intentions, I have gained more information about those people, I have not felt unduly obliged to alter significantly what had been written earlier. The characterizations that existed were fair and already did justice to those concerned...

Mr and Mrs Morgan are still rightly remembered proudly by their family, and thought well of by many others whose lives they touched. Although it was sad to discover that Miss Dickinson never did succeed in permanently securing the attention of Mr Owen (or any other suitor), it was good to discover that the Morgans' children went on to lead happy and fulfilling lives within a family that remained forever close to each other. Alun and Idris became successful dentists. Notably, when Idris invited his patients into his room for their dental treatment, he delighted in doing so with a measure of artistic flair... and finger pointing! Gly got married. Later, with her husband's help, she took over the running of the hotel. With the passing of the years, that responsibility has passed to their son.

It was entirely understandable that my mother looked forward, so much, to meeting the Morgans' children when they returned home on their holidays.

As befitting Gly's religious origins, she and her husband have set up an organisation that promotes international cultural co-operations and friendships. Her husband has ended up at least as well connected, honoured and important to their local community as Mr Morgan had been.

Gly's parents offered their home to several evacuees, possibly saving some of the children's lives – my mother's included. Now Gly and her husband have opened up the whole of Tenby as well, to the world. It was all entirely becoming…

A debt of gratitude goes to Alan Victor Broom and his wife, Christine. Alan's farm is pleasant, fine and modern. Nothing happens on it that could possibly upset a ten-year-old girl from London; for instance, no pigs are slaughtered there. However, Alan's long history of farming meant that he was able to provide plenty of invaluable technical information concerning agricultural practices in the 1940s. Consequently, I was able to add authentic period detail to my mother's story, of the agricultural environment in which she and her sister were depicted.

Another kind of thank you goes to my Uncle Ted, for giving my mother a place to stay just before she got married. Ted – a widower for many years – was a fine gentleman who spent most of his retirement in Norfolk. Unfortunately, he died in early 2009, having almost reached the age of ninety.

Finally, the deepest thanks go to my mother, who started this book, who co-wrote much of it and who gave me such a story to finish and the means by which to do it. It is to her and the many other ex-evacuees who were forever troubled by their wartime experiences – and those kind people who gave help, companionship and solace to the innocent, quiet casualties of war – that this book is respectfully dedicated.

Young Lillian

George,
Janice, Lilian,
her mother
Ellen, Stephen

The Last Evacuee is just one of a whole range
of publications from Y Lolfa. For a full list of
books currently in print, send now for your
free copy of our new full-colour catalogue.
Or simply surf into our website

www.ylolfa.com

for secure on-line ordering.

TALYBONT CEREDIGION CYMRU SY24 5HE
e-mail ylolfa@ylolfa.com
website www.ylolfa.com
phone (01970) 832 304
fax 832 782